OUR

NEXT

LIFE

A VIEW INTO THE
SPIRIT WORLD

GLEN W. PARK

OUR NEXT LIFE
A VIEW INTO THE SPIRIT WORLD

By Glen W. Park

Published by Vision, Inc.
Publications Division
P. O. Box 17181
Salt Lake City, UT 84117

ISBN: 978-0-9826076-0-2

Library of Congress Control Number: 2012951948

Cover Design by Anne P. Inouye

Cover Image by Dreamstime. Used by permission.

Printed in the United States of America

10 9 8 7 6 5 4 3 2 1

CONTENTS

ACKNOWLEDGMENTS

I wish to acknowledge the inspiration and assistance of many in the commencement and completion of this book.

The inspiration and communication from the Lord's Spirit from early on in my life led me to draw closer to Him and to study and ponder things of the Spirit. This effort brought even more inspiration and a greater testimony of His existence and love. The further result was a desire to continue to draw ever closer and to learn more about Him and His desires for me.

The comfort, inspiration and impressions of the Spirit during numerous difficult times in my life assured me of the Lord's continuing love and helped lead me to gain additional knowledge and faith, and to be more obedient and worthy.

My parents, brothers and sisters encouraged me to seek after good things and provided me opportunities to achieve and learn. The loss of my parents while I was young spurred me to search for answers to spiritual questions. The answers to those questions, received through the Holy Ghost, brought me peace and an increased desire to be faithful and obedient to the Lord.

My dear wife, Dianne, and my desire to share eternity with her, have been a continuing motivation to learn and live according to the Lord's will. Together, we have sought to turn our will over to His will in order to please Him and to be worthy of His great blessings.

My children have been a source of joy and motivation for me to live and strive to be better, to be able to share eternity with them.

I appreciate the assistance of my son, Craig, in helping me to review this book. I thank my daughter, Anne, for doing a superb job on the production of the cover of this book.

I return to my gratitude to the Lord. His miraculous preservation, restoration and extension of my life are wonderful beyond expression. These miracles and the lessons and growth they afforded, inspired me to complete this work in the hope that those who read it will be comforted and encouraged to work to receive the great blessing of dwelling among the righteous in *Our Next Life*—the spirit world.

GLEN W. PARK

INTRODUCTION
AND PURPOSE
OF THIS BOOK

. . . Eye hath not seen, nor ear heard, neither
have entered into the heart of man, the things
which God hath prepared for them that love him.[1]

And ye shall know the truth, and the truth
shall make you free.[2]

I have long been intrigued by the existence or life that follows
mortality. I am sure many others share that curiosity. I have studied
the scriptures and the writings of prophets and apostles, both ancient
and modern, in order to get a better view of what lies ahead, or in other
words, what kind of existence our next life will be.

As a teenager, my interest in the subject of our post–mortal
existence was probably similar to that of most teenagers who believe in
God. The subject is an interesting one for everyone, including
children, but it generally is really of no immediate concern. To a child,
the spirit world justifiably seems very far off. Even the thought of
adulthood appears to a child to be forever in the future.

In my later teenage years, I lost both of my parents, their deaths
occurring approximately three and a half months apart from each
other. I felt that most of my world was suddenly gone. My life would
never again be the same. I wondered how much my everyday
experiences would change. I searched for what my life was about and
considered my own mortality. I questioned what I should do with my
life and how much more difficult it would be without my parents. I
seriously searched, through study and prayer, for answers concerning
what was now happening to my parents. They were in the spirit world,

but what was it like there? What were they doing? Would I ever get to see them again? Were they happy? I felt I knew some of the answers but still wanted to know more. Those questions continued as I proceeded with my life. I completed high school, served a two-year mission for my church in Switzerland and France, married, obtained a bachelor's and doctoral degree and pursued my professional career as an attorney. My wife and I had six children and life was busy and generally happy, despite our share of trials.

Then, as a forty-year old, I, myself, began to have serious health problems. In the process of pleading with God and fighting to live, I experienced some very special spiritual experiences and received numerous answers to my pondering and prayers. Over an extended period of time, I have heard and read of the experiences of numerous others who underwent serious trials of varying types. I considered the hardships, the emotional and physical trauma and the sometimes devastating effects these difficult times brought to the lives and faith of so many others. I, therefore, determined I would write this book in an effort to provide truthful comfort, encouragement and assistance to others who must deal with the death of loved ones or their own mortality. What I have come to understand can be helpful for those who must endure trials and who fear those great unknowns—death and the life that follows this mortal one.

Every stage of our existence has been, and will be, of critical importance to our ultimate "forever" that lies ahead for each of us. Each stage has its own possibilities and requirements that must be accomplished in order for each of us to progress as far as possible in that stage and to reach the highest level in the stage that follows. Our degree of achievement and faithfulness in one stage determines at least somewhat where we begin the next stage of our eternal existence. On Earth, we can excel beyond our accomplishments in the pre–existence. In the world of spirits, we can continue to progress beyond where we left off on Earth. What we achieve in the spirit world—together with our level of faithfulness and progress in those prior existences—will determine the kingdom in which we will ultimately be judged worthy to dwell for the rest of eternity.

Although the spirit world, our life after mortality, may not technically be the most important stage of our existence, it is extremely important and is easily the most interesting right now—if for no other reason than that it is our next and lengthy destination after mortality. Normally, what lies right around the corner is more intriguing to us than what lies a considerable distance down the road. After all, if we do not correctly make it around the next corner, that changes the "what," "why" and "when" of that which lies farther down our road.

Furthermore, our knowledge and understanding of our next life in the spirit world can help us to make good decisions now while we are on Earth, that will determine in large part what we will experience and where in that realm we will find ourselves. Elder Orson Pratt said it well:

> . . . the more knowledge we get of the future, the more we impress it upon our minds and in our thoughts, the more we will be stirred up in our exertions to do that which concerns us at the present moment, knowing that it has an all-important bearing upon the future.[3]

With my intention being to increase our knowledge of, and improving the condition and happiness of, our future life, the primary purposes of this book are: (1) to testify of Jesus Christ, of God our Father and of the Holy Ghost; (2) to help others in understanding the spirit world; and (3) to help develop the desire in all of us to look forward with faith and hope to a marvelous experience that awaits us after this mortal life. This understanding can help us determine now to strive harder to be faithful to Christ and to follow His commandments more diligently. For, by so doing, we will better insure that our experiences in the spirit world will be wonderful, for we will have done those things the Lord Jesus Christ has stated are necessary to receive the great blessings He has promised to those who are faithful to Him; and finally, (4) to do all of the above in a short, easy-to-read format so that anyone can understand what awaits us all after mortality and what type of individuals we must become to receive the types of blessings there that we desire to obtain.

I begin with my personal witness. I testify that Jesus Christ is the divine and perfect Son of God, and the Savior and Redeemer of the world. I also testify of His Father, and our Father in Heaven, the Great God, Elohim. He loved us so much that He gave His only Begotten Son to suffer and to die for us, that thereby we all might be eternally blessed. I am grateful for the Holy Ghost, the third member of the Godhead. His primary roles are to bear witness of God our Father and of His Son, to provide comfort and peace and to reveal all truth. Part of His testifying of them is bearing witness of the plan of salvation, of our relationship with God, our Father, and with His Son, Jesus Christ—which relationships began in the pre-existence, and that have the potential to continue through the eternities.

Understanding the spirit world and its place in our Father's plan of salvation for all of us will give us encouragement and hope. This understanding and knowledge will relieve our fear of death and will also help those who have lost, or will hereafter lose, loved ones to death. The knowledge and understanding of what awaits good people who die can greatly bless and lift those who mourn for deceased loved ones. Those who mourn deserve to receive this comfort, for the truth can even free them from pain, questions and worry over their loved ones who have passed on.

I have included as the basis for my descriptions of the world of spirits, three types of sources:

1. Pronouncements and writings of apostles and prophets, both ancient and modern;

2. Accounts of other faithful men and women who have had personal experiences, either by vision or by actual out-of-body visits, to the spirit realm. Although these accounts are not canonized, they conform to what apostles and prophets have written and said. They

add non-contradictory and informative details that further enlighten and expand our understanding of the places, inhabitants and circumstances of the spirit world. They also add personal touches and feelings that assist us in these views into the next life that awaits us. Their accounts are extraordinary, both in their inspirational value and intellectual content. Furthermore, they do complement and support the writings of apostles and prophets presented herein; and

3. Promptings of the Spirit, that are truthful and that I believe to be accurate concerning this great place where we will all go in the near and not-so-near future.

I have primarily used the pronouncements and writings of apostles and prophets in this book. Those pronouncements and writings are doctrinally correct. I believe in the statement of the ancient prophet Amos, found in the Old Testament, that assures us, **"Surely God will do nothing, save He shall reveal His secrets to His servants, the prophets."**[4]

It is my firm belief and testimony that the Lord Jesus Christ anciently did this, but also that He still does work by that promise of His, spoken through the mouth of one of His prophets. In other words, I believe with all my heart, and I testify to you, that the Lord Jesus Christ, which God is the same yesterday, today and forever, does still speak through the mouths of His prophets.

Many of the most profound, far-reaching and instructive descriptions of the worlds to come, both of the spirit world and of the kingdoms that follow our resurrection and final judgment, come from the writings and pronouncements of the modern apostles and prophets who received their authority as a result of the reestablishment of the Church of Jesus Christ, which followed the calling and bestowal of such authority to that modern-day prophet, Joseph Smith.

This book is written for the benefit of everyone who reads it. It is not written to be understandable only to the religious scholar. It is written to be understood by virtually anyone—those of every spiritual level, and even for those who are searching for a basic understanding of the things of God. For those with a great knowledge of gospel truths, some of the preliminary topics discussed will not contain new or unusual information. Those earlier topics will reinforce and remind us all of the great plan of salvation of our God and will be a healthy preface for the discussion of the things that will then follow.

My sincere desire is that in this book, the reader will find truths which will encourage, uplift and inspire each to live more as Christ taught we should live. By so doing, the reader can bring himself or herself to a higher level of worthiness and closeness to the Lord. Doing so will result in a greater perfecting of the individual. If this is the result, I will be most happy, and the purposes for which this book is written will have been fulfilled.

For the reader to better understand the world of spirits that awaits each of us following our mortal life, we will first put into proper perspective this spirit realm.

Therefore, we will first briefly discuss the pre–existence, the realm where we dwelt with God, our Father, and with our Elder Brother, Jesus, before coming to this Earth. We will also discuss the purposes of our mortal life, and then those events that follow our sojourn in the spirit world: namely, the resurrection and our assignment to one of several kingdoms, followed by the final judgment which will determine where we will dwell for the rest of forever.

Obviously, because the discussion of each of these realms could by itself consume volumes, I will only briefly write about each of these places and how they relate to each other in the overall scheme of things—in our eternal existence.

Keeping in mind the expressed purposes for which this book is written, I desire that this work be short enough to be easily read and understood by all. If that be the case, there is a better prospect that more will be lifted and inspired to be closer to the Lord and to live according to His teachings. More may receive hope in the hereafter and make of themselves better sons and daughters of God. More will be encouraged and given hope concerning this world of spirits, both for themselves and their loved ones.

CHAPTER 1

THE PLAN OF SALVATION

To understand why trials and suffering are allowed, and even necessary in mortality, it is helpful to understand how this part of our longer existence—this mortality—fits into the rest of our eternity. After all, mortality is literally only an extremely small part of that longer existence that spans eons of time prior to mortality and will span additional eons of time—even forever—after our life on Earth.

I here concisely list the various parts of that long existence:

Pre-existence as spirit children of God the Father;

Passing through a veil of forgetfulness—temporarily removing all memory of our pre-existence;

Birth into mortality—the uniting of our pre-existing spirit with a new mortal (physical) body;

Mortality—life on Earth—where we are tested and can develop physically, emotionally and spiritually;

Death—the separation of our spirit from our mortal (physical) body;

Spirit World—divided into paradise for the righteous, and spirit prison for the wicked of numerous and varying degrees;

Assignment to a kingdom of glory for most, or perdition for the extremely evil;

Resurrection—the reuniting of our spirit to our body that will then be immortal;

Final Judgment—where the Lord judges each individual as to the totality of our personality and disposition and as to what each has become, based upon our obedience to divine law and the development of our character;

Life throughout the rest of eternity in the kingdom we have inherited through the atonement of Christ and according to our faith, obedience and good works.

Let us briefly look at each part of our existence, with extra emphasis being given to what awaits us in the spirit world.

CHAPTER 2

THE PRE-EXISTENCE AS SPIRIT CHILDREN OF GOD

At some point, each of us became a spirit child of God our Father. We dwelled with God for an extended period. He came to know each of us very well.

We are told in the Book of Hebrews:

> Furthermore we have had fathers of our flesh
> which corrected us, and we gave them reverence: shall
> we not much rather be in subjection unto the Father of
> spirits, and live?[5]

This reference speaks to our having a spirit Father. That is God, our Father in Heaven, the Father of our spirits.

Christ, before coming to Earth as the child of Mary and God, appeared to a righteous, mortal man and spoke of His own spirit body—not His body of flesh that He would later receive. Christ said:

> Behold, this body, which ye now behold, is the
> body of my spirit; and man have I created after the body
> of my spirit; and even as I appear unto thee to be in the
> spirit will I appear unto my people in the flesh.[6]

For anyone to properly understand this doctrine of pre-existence, it will be helpful for me to explain a few fundamental truths: (1) God our Father is a real, personal Being with a physical body; (2) He is an exalted and perfect Being who possesses a tangible, immortal body; (3) Mortal man was created in His image; (4) All matter existed, is eternal and was not created out of nothing; (5) The creation of everything pertaining to this Earth, was an organization or reorganization of that existing matter; (6) The purposes of our coming to Earth are two-fold: (a) to receive a physical body; and (b) to learn, develop, and progress in order to become like God.

We learn, develop and progress through exercising God-given agency. Agency is His gift to us, bestowing the right to choose the path we will follow during our pre-Earth, Earth, and post-Earth existences. God gave us the power to choose to obey or to choose to disobey His commandments. We need to understand that this agency allows us to choose a course of action which automatically comes with natural consequences. Agency does not allow us to choose a course of action plus a consequence that is inconsistent with that initial choice.

Therefore, if we choose a path that leads to happiness and eternal good, that is what we will receive (if not always immediately, at least eternally.) If we choose a disobedient path, we get the natural consequences thereof. Most disobedient people feel they are entitled to choose wickedness and yet reap blissful results. But as the prophet Alma taught his son, Corianton, "... Behold, I say unto you, wickedness never was happiness."[7]

The fact is, God's eternal commandments are intended to enable us to attain happiness by doing the things whose consequence is progress and happiness. Those commandments are also intended to persuade us to not do the things whose consequence is decline, unhappiness or misery. An illustration makes this concept easy for children and adults alike to understand:

If one obeys his parents and does not touch a hot coil of the kitchen range, he remains pain-free. If he disobeys and touches that hot coil, he experiences severe physical limitation and pain for an extended period of time. The parent, being wiser and more experienced, **knows ahead of time what the consequence of that particular action will be**. The parent does not choose or want the consequence of disobedience to be extremely painful. But it simply is.

Like that parent, our heavenly Parent **knows ahead of time what the consequence of every particular action will be**. God does not choose or want the consequence of disobedience to be painful or miserable. But it simply is. ". . . [W]ickedness never was happiness."[8]

Some spirit children choose to obey and to closely follow the directions—commandments—of our all-knowing and kind Father. Others choose to disobey or neglect to follow Him, and therefore, accomplish very little. The Lord showed Abraham the state and level of the intelligences and spirits that dwelled with God our Father.

> Now the Lord had shown unto me, Abraham, the intelligences that were organized before the world was; and among all these there were many of the noble and great ones;
>
> And God saw these souls that they were good, and he stood in the midst of them, and he said: These I will make my rulers; for he stood among those that were spirits, and he saw that they were good; and he said unto me: Abraham, thou art one of them; thou wast chosen before thou wast born.
>
> And there stood one among them that was like unto God, and he said unto those who were with him: We will go down, for there is space there, and we will take of these materials, and we will make an earth whereon these may dwell;

11

> And we will prove them herewith, to see if they will
> do all things whatsoever the Lord their God shall command
> them;[9]

It is worth noting that the term "rulers" refers to leaders of God's kingdom on Earth, not to secular or worldly rulers. Many world leaders have been, and are, unworthy to be leaders in God's kingdom on Earth.

There were vast differences in the level of progress of the numerous intelligences that existed. Some were nearly like God—such as Jesus Christ—and some were not good enough to even accept God's plan of salvation and to come to Earth (e.g. Lucifer and his followers.) Some of those who chose to follow Jesus Christ (Jehovah) were very noble and great (e.g. Abraham), and some were extremely self–centered, proud and evil (e.g. Hitler and Stalin.) Most of the others were somewhere in between. Thus we see the need for varied levels of rewards in the hereafter.

CHAPTER 3

THE VEIL
BETWEEN THE
PRE-EXISTENCE
AND MORTALITY

A short but vital part of the great plan of salvation of God is our passing through a "veil of forgetfulness." If our progress in mortality is to be based upon faith—and it is—then it is essential that we forget our pre-existent life with God our Father. Why? If we knew here all we had experienced there, faith would be unnecessary. The prophet Alma said it this way:

> Now I ask, is this faith? Behold, I say unto you,
> Nay; for if a man knoweth a thing he hath no cause to
> believe, for he knoweth it.[10]

The Lord speaks of this trial of our faith through the prophet Zechariah, who said:

And I will bring the third part through the fire, and
will refine them as silver is refined, and will try them as
gold is tried: they shall call on my name, and I will hear them:
I will say, It is my people: and they shall say, The
LORD is my God.[11]

The veil and our forgetting are also referred to in Ecclesiastes
and Isaiah, as follows:

There is no remembrance of former things; neither
shall there be any remembrance of things that are to come
with those that shall come after.[12]

And he will destroy in this mountain the face of the
covering cast over all people, and the vail (sic) that is spread
over all nations.[13]

CHAPTER 4

MORTALITY

The ultimate purpose of God's great plan of salvation is to give us the opportunity to progress in all ways necessary to become as God is. God, our Father, has a perfected, immortal body. In the pre-existence, we had only spirit bodies, lacking a physical body. So an obvious step in becoming like our Father—God—we would need to have a physical body. Hence, one of the primary purposes of mortality is to gain a physical body.

The next important purposes of mortality can be summed up by this short list:

(1) To gain the experience life presents;

(2) To learn many things—especially important truths;

(3) To have our spirit gain control over our physical body;

(4) To progress and improve ourselves;

(5) To be deemed by God worthy—through Christ's atonement—to receive the rewards and blessings He has promised those who are obedient to His commandments;

(6) To become as God is.

We are even commanded: **"Be ye therefore perfect, even as your Father which is in heaven is perfect."**[14]

Doing so will obviously take conscious and continued effort. Even though as imperfect mortals we will not become perfect while on Earth, we can come to a higher level of goodness, valiance and obedience, so that we will not have a long distance to go to finish the process in our next stage of existence—the spirit world.

CHAPTER 5

THE SPIRIT WORLD: A BRIEF INTRODUCTION

Following our departure from mortality through death, our spirit, separated from our mortal body, returns to a spirit realm, the spirit world. There, we will continue in our process of progressing, digressing or maintaining the level of wickedness, goodness or godliness that we had attained on Earth. We will enter that post–mortal existence in precisely the same state of mind and with precisely the same attitude and character we had when we left the mortal existence. The prophet Alma says it well:

> Ye cannot say, when ye are brought to that awful crisis, that I will repent, that I will return to my God. Nay, ye cannot say this; for that same spirit which doth possess your bodies at the time that ye go out of this life, that same spirit will have power to possess your body in that eternal world.[15]

In the spirit world, we will possess the same disposition that makes us who and what we are on the Earth. On the other side of the veil of death, we will be as we entered the spirit world, exactly the same person, with exactly the same desires, appetites, intentions, wants, aspirations, character, dispositions and moods that we had just moments before as we dwelled in our last days on Earth. We will, entering the spirit world, be the sum total of what we became on Earth. If we did not amount to much on Earth—not by worldly standards, but as far as our true character and personality—we will enter the spirit world at no higher level.

Brigham Young explained well how individuals will be:

> Suppose, then, that a man is evil in his heart— wholly given up to wickedness, and in that condition dies, his spirit will enter into the spirit world intent upon evil. On the other hand, if we are striving with all the powers and faculties God has given us to improve upon our talents, to prepare ourselves to dwell in eternal life, and the grave receives our bodies while we are thus engaged, with what disposition will our spirits enter their next state? They will be still striving to do the things of God, only in a much greater degree—learning, increasing, growing in grace and in the knowledge of the truth.[16]

God, our Father, will continue to preserve our agency. If we chose to be good on the Earth, He will not take away from us that choice. If we chose to be evil, He will leave us to remain evil, even though He certainly would like for us to have chosen to be good.

In the spirit world, we will continue to have the opportunity to progress, to become more like God. Some will indeed use this opportunity to progress and will do so. Others will choose instead to remain lazy, rebellious, or both. Unless they choose to change, they will not progress much and will continue to be unhappy and poor in character.

CHAPTER 6

THE RESURRECTION

Following an extended period of time in the spirit world, all will ultimately be resurrected. The Apostle John explains:

> Marvel not at this: for the hour is coming, in the
> which all that are in the graves shall hear his voice,
> And shall come forth; they that have done good,
> unto the resurrection of life; and they that have done
> evil, unto the resurrection of damnation.[17]

At death, our spirits separate from our physical bodies. At the resurrection, each spirit will be reunited with its body. Only that body will not be a mortal, corrupted, or corruptible one. The individual elements of each person's body, however and wherever they had been laid to rest or scattered will all come together to form an immortal body. It will never again be subject to death, illness, pain or physical suffering. This immortal body is Christ's gift to each individual who has ever lived on Earth. This is what is sometimes referred to as the universal salvation given to man by God.

Through the atoning grace of the Lord, then based upon personal worthiness, level of progression and obedience, individuals will be placed in some level of glorified body. The only exceptions will be those who the Lord judges to be evil enough to be sent to perdition. There will be a vast range in the glory of bodies given to individuals.

The range of glory will be based upon the vast difference in the types of character those individuals had developed during the prior existences—pre-existence as spirit children of God, mortality and spirit world.

The Old Testament prophet Hosea wrote of the power the Lord will have to resurrect everyone who lived upon the Earth.

> I will ransom them from the power of the grave;
> I will redeem them from death: O death, I will be thy
> plagues; O grave, I will be thy destruction: repentance
> shall be hid from mine eyes.[18]

The Apostle Paul succinctly said it: "As in Adam all die, even so in Christ shall all be made alive."[19]

As quoted above, the Apostle John expresses it this way:

> Marvel not at this: for the hour is coming, in the
> which all that are in the graves shall hear his voice,
> And shall come forth; they that have done good,
> unto the resurrection of life; and they that have done
> evil, unto the resurrection of damnation.[20]

This resurrection is the universal salvation that comes through the grace of the Lord Jesus Christ. Everyone ever born into mortality will be resurrected. But all who are resurrected will not be rejoined with their Father in Heaven. Many will be resurrected with bodies unworthy to be in His divine presence. Only those who have become sufficiently like Him will be able to be with Him. That reward—exaltation—is the crowning part of salvation and is also available only through the grace of Christ. For His great and eternal atonement will open the way for us to repent and receive forgiveness of our sins, which forgiveness "erases" them from our life.

CHAPTER 7

ASSIGNMENT TO A KINGDOM OF GLORY

Not every one that saith unto me, Lord, Lord, shall
enter into the kingdom of heaven; but he that doeth the
will of my Father which is in heaven."[21]

Following the universal resurrection, each individual will be
assigned to that place of which he is deserving, based upon his
faithfulness, obedience, valiance, and good works. I must stress that in
reality, except for Jesus Christ only, not one of us who has ever lived
on Earth, in and of ourselves, deserves any of the levels of glory that
await us in any of the kingdoms to come. Only through the grace of
Christ, accomplished through His atonement and death, will we have
the opportunity to be cleansed from our sins. Only through the
atoning blood of Christ—which will result in our being made purer
than we ever could have otherwise been—can the Lord and our Father
in Heaven look upon us as worthy to return to their presence. This is
the greatest evidence of the unmatched love, patience and caring that
God our Father and His Divine Son have for us.

I will now give a brief description of each of the three
kingdoms of glory to which resurrected children of God will go, and of

perdition, that realm reserved for those who continued to consciously rebel against God, even until the end.

CELESTIAL KINGDOM

The Celestial Kingdom is the highest and most glorious of all kingdoms. It is where God our Father dwells. It, obviously, is a wonderful and beautiful place.

The people who will go there are they who received a testimony of Jesus Christ, the Son of God, and were valiant in that testimony. They believed and exercised faith in Him. The Doctrine and Covenants tells us that they were baptized:

> . . . after the manner of his burial, being buried in the water in his name, and this according to the commandment which he has given. . . . Wherefore, all things are theirs, whether life or death, or things present, or things to come, all are theirs and they are Christ's, and Christ is God's.
>
> And they shall overcome all things. . . . These shall dwell in the presence of God and his Christ forever and ever.[22]

On January 21, 1836, the prophet Joseph Smith received a revelation that further explained who would, through the atonement of Jesus Christ, qualify for the celestial kingdom:

> All who have died without a knowledge of the gospel, who would have received it if they had been permitted to tarry, shall be heirs of the celestial kingdom

of God; also all that shall die henceforth without a knowledge of it, who would have received it with all their hearts, shall be heirs of that kingdom, for I, the Lord, will judge all men according to their works, according to the desire of their hearts.[23]

Elder Joseph Fielding Smith added these comments about the above revelation to the prophet Joseph:

One very significant thing in this revelation, which should be remembered, is the fact that the Lord did not say that all who are dead are entitled to these blessings in the celestial kingdom, if they hear the gospel in the spirit world, but all who would have received the gospel had they been given the opportunity in this mortal life. *The privilege of exaltation is not held out to those who have had the opportunity to receive Christ and obey his truth and who have refused to do so.*[24]

Elder Smith further expounded upon the subject as follows:

The justice of the Lord is manifest in the right he grants to all men to hear the plan of salvation and receive it. Some have that privilege in this life; if they obey the gospel, well and good; if they reject it, then in the spirit world the same opportunities with the same fullness do not come to them.

If they die without that opportunity in this life, it will reach them in the world of spirits. The gospel will there be declared to them, and if they are willing to accept it, it is counted unto them just the same as if they had embraced it in mortality. In this way justice is meted out to every man; all are placed on an equality before the bar of God.[25]

Elder Bruce R. McConkie explained the meaning of valiance in one's testimony of Jesus:

> To be valiant in the testimony of Jesus is to bridle our passions, control our appetites, and rise above carnal and evil things. It is to overcome the world as did he who is our prototype and who himself was the most valiant of all our Father's children. It is to be morally clean, to pay our tithes and offerings, to honor the Sabbath day, to pray with full purpose of heart, to lay our all upon the altar if called upon to do so.
>
> To be valiant in the testimony of Jesus is to take the Lord's side on every issue. It is to vote as he would vote. It is to think what he thinks, to believe what he believes, to say what he would say and do what he would do in the same situation. It is to have the mind of Christ and be one with him as he is one with his Father.[26]

This is a place where no one need worry about being with or around evil people who refuse to repent—murderers, liars, adulterers, abusers, bullies, etc. Why? Because none of them will be permitted to be there. They will never reach that high place of glory.

TERRESTRIAL KINGDOM

The terrestrial kingdom is the middle or next-to-the-highest kingdom. It is a very nice place—although not nearly as nice as the celestial kingdom. Next to the celestial, the terrestrial kingdom would be as the moon compared with the sun, obviously not nearly as glorious or great.

Those who go to the Terrestrial Kingdom have not been valiant in the testimony of Jesus, so they do not warrant the Celestial Kingdom, where Christ and God the Father dwell.

These are good, honorable people, "who were blinded by the craftiness of men."[27]

Elder Joseph Fielding Smith explained how the Lord's justice works concerning those who go to the terrestrial kingdom as a continuation of the quotation on those who qualify for the celestial kingdom. Of those to be assigned to the terrestrial kingdom, he said:

> Those who have the opportunity here, those unto whom the message of salvation is declared, who are taught and who have this truth presented to them in this life—yet who deny it and refuse to receive it—shall not have a place in the kingdom of God. They will not be those who died without that knowledge and who yet accepted it in the spirit world.[28]

Elder James E. Talmage also taught on this subject:

> The gifts of God are not confined to this sphere of action, but will be bestowed in justice throughout eternity. Upon all who reject the word of God in this life will fall the penalties provided; but after the debt has been paid the prison doors shall be opened, and the spirits once confined in suffering, then chastened and clean, shall come forth to partake of the glory provided for their class.[29]

He further clarified in a statement that applies to inheritors of both the terrestrial and telestial kingdoms: "Deliverance from hell is not admittance to heaven [meaning the celestial kingdom]."[30]

Elder Joseph Fielding Smith also taught:

> Into the terrestrial kingdom will go all those who are honorable and who have lived clean virtuous lives, but who would not receive the Gospel, but in the spirit world repented and accepted it as far as it can be given unto them. Many of these have been blinded by tradition and the love of the world, and have not been able to see the beauties of the Gospel.[31]

Joseph Fielding Smith said:

> After the Lord and the righteous who are caught up to meet him have descended upon the earth, there will come to pass another resurrection. This may be considered as a part of the first, although it comes later. In this resurrection will come forth those of the terrestrial order, who were not worthy to be caught up to meet him, but who are worthy to come forth to enjoy the millennial reign.[32]

These people are good individuals, but, because of their lack of valiance to the Lord Jesus Christ, they are limited in their eternal progress and advancement. They will be eternally happier than those of the next, lower kingdom. That is because this kingdom "excels in all things the glory of the telestial."[33]

TELESTIAL KINGDOM

The telestial kingdom is a kingdom of glory. In fact, the Lord declared that the glory of the telestial "surpasses all understanding."[34] But, it is the lowest in glory—far below either of the others. Think of its glory being as the brightness of a star compared with that of the moon, from the vantage point of the Earth. That is the comparison of the glory of this lowest kingdom of glory to the middle kingdom. Then, think of its glory being as a star, compared to the noonday sun. That is the comparison of this lowest kingdom's glory to the highest, the celestial kingdom. That is an immense difference.

Its inhabitants are described in The Doctrine and Covenants:

> These are they who are liars, and sorcerers, and adulterers, and whoremongers, and whosoever loves and makes a lie.[35]
> These will . . . suffer the wrath of Almighty God until the fulness of times, when Christ shall have subdued all enemies under his feet, and shall have perfected his work;
> When he shall deliver up the kingdom, and present it unto the Father, spotless, . . .
> Then shall he (Christ) be crowned with the crown of his glory, to sit on the throne of his power to reign forever and ever. . . .
> . . . but where God and Christ dwell they cannot come, worlds without end.[36]

Just as the glory, or brightness, of one star in the sky differs from that of other stars, so the glory of the individuals who inherit the telestial kingdom shall differ from one another. The scriptural description of such differences is:

> . . . the glory and the inhabitants of the telestial
> world, [are] . . . as innumerable as the stars in the
> firmament of heaven, or as the sand upon the seashore;[37]

Why will there be so many different levels of glory or reward in this lowest kingdom of glory? The differences in levels of goodness, badness and wickedness of people vary greatly. Let us consider just a few examples of unrepentant sinners.

Compare the relative wickedness of one who physically abuses others with someone who lies. Certainly neither individual is a sterling character. Both are wicked, but the degree of wickedness is quite different, one from the other.

Now consider someone who has stolen a few small things but who refuses to reform himself—to repent. Compare him to one who has stolen millions of dollars from others and has not repented.

Compare one who beats up on others with one who has murdered multiple people. Again, both are wicked, but one has not reached the greater level of wickedness of the other.

There are a myriad of types of evil that man may choose to pursue, exercising the agency given by God, and many will indeed choose from among those multiple levels of wickedness available.

Obviously, the types of unsavory characters described in this brief set of comparisons are all individuals around whom I do not want to be for the rest of forever. Just the thought of that prospect should cause each of us to do that which is necessary—to repent and make whatever changes in our lives—to be able to avoid being consigned to that type of environment and company forever!

PERDITION

I will now give a short description of the lowest dwelling place for those who have come to Earth—perdition.

We are told that they—those who are sent to perdition—are "the only ones on whom the second death shall have any power."[38] The first death is physical. Even the very evil men will be resurrected. Therefore, they will not forever remain subject to that first death.

The "second death" refers to a spiritual death, that is, an unending, everlasting separation from God the Father, from His Son, Jesus Christ, and from ministering angels sent by them or by their authorized administrators.

Those evil enough to be sent to perdition will forever be without the blessing of the presence of God the Father, of Jesus Christ, of the Holy Ghost, and even of the ministrations of those who inherit any of these above-described kingdoms of glory. In other words, they will forever be without the company of, or the spiritual "lift" of anyone who could bring with them the buoying up or enlightening gifts of a spiritual nature. That is, they shall remain subject to evil as they became following Satan, because they voluntarily subjected themselves to him during mortality, and never became better during the entire period of the millennium. "These will not be redeemed in the due time of the Lord after the sufferings of this wrath."[39] They will receive resurrected, immortal bodies, but will remain in their filthy, evil condition for the rest of eternity.

All those who inherit the Celestial, Terrestrial or Telestial Kingdoms will be in a kingdom of glory. But those who are judged unworthy of even the lowest level of the lowest of those kingdoms of glory shall be cast down to perdition.

They are they . . . of whom I say that it had been
better for them never to have been born;

28

For they are vessels of wrath, doomed to suffer the wrath of God, with the devil and his angels in eternity;

Concerning whom I have said there is no forgiveness in this world nor in the world to come—

Having denied the Holy Spirit after having received it, and having denied the Only Begotten Son of the Father, having crucified him unto themselves and put him to an open shame.

These are they who shall go away into the lake of fire and brimstone, with the devil and his angels—

And the only ones on whom the second death shall have any power.[40]

CHAPTER 8

THE FINAL
JUDGMENT

Jesus Christ is the same wonderful being through whose grace (1) we will be resurrected, and (2) we can repent, be forgiven of our sins and be made pure enough—through the grace of Christ—to qualify to return to God our Father. Christ will be the Great Judge who will assign us to a kingdom of glory according to our own individual works and what we become on Earth and in the spirit world.

The Apostle John said: "For the Father judgeth no man, but hath committed all judgment unto the Son."[41]

This is certainly appropriate and wonderful for us. He who suffered and died for us because of his overwhelming love will be He who also judges us. He will determine if we have sincerely repented to take advantage of His infinite and eternal atonement—the condition He has set to have our sins forgiven—even washed clean.

The everlasting result of the final judgment for us will be the reward we receive for the type of lives we have lived and the quality of person we have become. In other words, we will be judged on our obedience, the valiance of our testimony in keeping the commandments of the Lord and the service we rendered to our fellow men and to Jesus Christ, the Lord.

The scriptures refer to the "coming of the great and dreadful day of the Lord."[42] How is it both great <u>and</u> dreadful? For the righteous, His second coming will be a great and marvelous day. They will be caught up to meet Him as He returns in majesty and power.

For the wicked, Christ's coming in power will be something they dread. Because of their evil and rebellious lives, they will be destroyed from off the face of the Earth. There will be a vast multitude of wicked swept off the Earth and sent to the place in the spirit world that awaits them—spirit prison. There, they will be conscious of their unworthiness before the Lord.

We can all be certain the initial judgment—that occurs as every individual leaves mortality and enters the spirit world—and the final judgment—that occurs as every individual departs the spirit world to forever dwell in the kingdom to which he or she has been assigned, will be just. Because Christ loves everyone—even to the laying down His life for us—His judgment will be well beyond just. We will receive much more than we, individually, deserve. Through His atoning sacrifice and death on Calvary, He voluntarily paid the heavy price for our sins—on condition of our individual repentance. As He has told us through the prophet Isaiah: ". . . though your sins be as scarlet, they shall be white as snow; though they be like crimson, they shall be as wool.[43]

That transformation, the cleansing of our sinful souls through the blood of Christ, can result in our being considered by God as free of sin—worthy to return to His glorious presence. How, exactly, is it done? Countless religious men and women, scholars and unlearned, have asked that question and sought its answer. May I simply say that through God, all things are possible. Because of His perfection, His unconditional love and His omnipotence, His suffering and death alone could bring about such a cleansing. And He has! We all are, or can be, the beneficiaries of His magnificent atonement and the wonderful blessings that eternally may be ours if we take advantage of His selfless offer to repent and come unto Him.[44]

CHAPTER 9

RETURN TO A PRIOR STAGE—THE FOCUS OF THIS BOOK—THE SPIRIT WORLD

Having previously skipped our detailed view into the spirit world, we will now take our view back there.

We will first look at the process of leaving mortality and traveling to the world of spirits.

Our view of the spirit world will next look at general aspects of that wonderful place for a vast number of the spirits who will go there. This will include many interesting and revealing insights into this next realm for men and women who have lived upon the Earth.

Then we will view the activities of the wicked in spirit prison, which are not so wonderful. This will be followed by our view of the less wicked—let us say—uncommitted spirits in spirit prison.

Finally, we will view paradise—a glorious place for those who have strived in mortality to live as the Lord has asked us all to live.

OUTLINE OF THE CHAPTERS TO FOLLOW

The field is the world; the good seed are the children of the kingdom; but the tares are the children of the wicked one;

The enemy that sowed them is the devil; the harvest is the end of the world; and the reapers are the angels.

As therefore the tares are gathered and burned in the fire; so shall it be in the end of this world.

The Son of man shall send forth his angels, and they shall gather out of his kingdom all things that offend, and them which do iniquity;

And shall cast them into a furnace of fire: there shall be wailing and gnashing of teeth.

Then shall the righteous shine forth as the sun in the kingdom of their Father.

Who hath ears to hear, let him hear.[45]

Again, the kingdom of heaven is like unto a net, that was cast into the sea, and gathered of every kind:

Which, when it was full, they drew to shore, and sat down, and gathered the good into vessels, but cast the bad away.

So shall it be at the end of the world: the angels shall come forth, and sever the wicked from among the just,

And shall cast them into the furnace of fire: there shall be wailing and gnashing of teeth.

Jesus saith unto them, Have ye understood all these things? They say unto him, Yea, Lord.[46]

I am excited to be able to now discuss with some detail the primary focus of this book—the world of spirits, or spirit world. Our discussion of the world of spirits will be divided into several parts, each in its own chapter. Of course, there will be some repetition, since a description of one part of the spirit world will overlap into the description of other parts. Furthermore, the description of the various parts of this realm will be further divided into sub-parts.

The different aspects of the spirit world we will view are these:

1. What we will likely experience on the way as we enter the spirit world, immediately following our death.

2. What the spirit world looks like. This will have the following sub-sections:

> A. General aspects of the spirit world.
> B. The place where at least two different levels of wicked go to dwell, pending the resurrection: (i) those who are relatively good, but not committed to Christ; and (ii) those who are evil.
> C. The gulf, or dividing line, between where the wicked and where the righteous dwell.
> D. The place where the righteous go to dwell, pending their resurrection.

3. The kinds of activities of spirits in the spirit world.

> A. The activities of the wicked—in varying degrees of wickedness.
> B. The activities of the righteous—in varying degrees of righteousness and preparedness.

4. What people (spirits) look like in the spirit world.

CHAPTER 10

THE SPIRIT WORLD

A GENERAL VIEW

President Joseph F. Smith discussed the subject of man's departure from mortality into the spirit world. He stated:

> The spirits of all men, as soon as they depart from this mortal body, whether they are good or evil, . . . are taken home to that God who gave them life, where there is a separation, a partial judgment, and the spirits of those who are righteous are received into a state of happiness which is called paradise, a state of rest, a state of peace, where they expand in wisdom, where they have respite from all their troubles, and where care and sorrow do not annoy.
>
> The wicked, on the contrary, have no part nor portion in the Spirit of the Lord, and they are cast into outer darkness, being led captive, because of their own iniquity, by the evil one.
>
> And in this space between death and the resurrection of the body, the two classes of souls remain, in happiness or in misery, until the time which is appointed of God that the

35

dead shall come forth and be reunited both spirit and body, and be brought to stand before God, and be judged according to their works. This is the final judgment.[47]

In 1st Peter, we learn that Christ was quickened by the Spirit:

By which also he went and preached unto the spirits in prison;
Which sometime were disobedient, . . .[48]

At the time of our mortal death, we will pass through a second veil. This veil has also been called a "film" through which the spirit of each individual passes, having just left the mortal body on Earth. This passing through not just the veil, but <u>to</u> the spirit world takes but a very short time, perhaps only a fraction of a second—and we are there—or here, as it were, in a realm that is comprised of an area which encompasses and even includes this Earth. We are just in a different part of this space. We are in a different state or form and so we can occupy much of the same overall space, because we actually occupy a different part, element or sphere of the Earth's environment—the spirit sphere rather than the physical sphere.

What, then, prevents us, as mortals, from seeing the spirits who inhabit the same Earth that we inhabit? When our spirits separate from their earthly bodies, as spirits they are capable of seeing, hearing and doing spiritual things. And where are these spirits going to be doing, seeing and hearing such things? Right here, in this same system that the Lord created for us to come to and receive our physical bodies. We cannot see the spiritual realm with our mortal eyes, but it is all around us. The following will help to explain how this can be.

We read in chapter 6 of 2nd Kings, that the king of Syria was employing his army, seeking to defeat Israel. But everywhere he sent his troops, Israel's army was ready and waiting. Syria's army continually lost battles to the army of Israel. Finally, Syria's king had had enough. He suspected a traitor within his own inner circle.

The king of Syria asked:

> Will ye not shew me which of us is for the king of Israel?
> And one of his servants said, None, my lord, O king: but Elisha, the prophet that is in Israel, telleth the king of Israel the words that thou speakest in thy bedchamber.[49]

So the king of Syria turned his wrath against the prophet Elisha. He found where Elisha was and sent a great host of his army with their horses and chariots. By night, they surrounded Dothan, the city where Elisha and his servant were staying.

Early in the morning, the servant of Elisha rose and beheld the great host surrounding the entire city. Worried, Elisha's servant asked what they could do?

Elisha reassured him, saying:

> Fear not: for they that be with us are more than they that be with them.
> And Elisha prayed, and said, Lord, I pray thee, open his eyes, that he may see. And the Lord opened the eyes of the young man; and he saw: and, behold, the mountain was full of horses and chariots of fire round about Elisha.[50]

Just as the Lord changed and improved the perception of the mortal, natural eyes of the servant of Elisha, He could change our eyes so we would be able to see spirits as clearly as we can now see the natural, mortal bodies of those around us on the Earth. Without such change provided by the Lord or His Spirit, mortal eyes are unable to see spirits who are around us.

One of the first impressions one will likely have upon arriving in the realm of the spirit world could be the very nearness of the place.

It is not millions of miles away from Earth. Nor is it even thousands or hundreds of miles distant. President Joseph F. Smith stated:

> It is not beyond the sun, but is on this earth that was organized for the people that have lived and that do and will live upon it. No other people can have it, and we can have no other kingdom until we are prepared to inhabit this eternally.[51]

Brigham Young declared:

> When you lay down this tabernacle, where are you going? Into the spiritual world. . . . Where is the spirit world? It is right here. Do the good and evil spirits go together? Yes they do. . . . Do they go beyond the boundaries of the organized Earth? No, they do not. . . .
> Can you see it with your natural eyes? No. Can you see spirits in this room? No. Suppose the Lord should touch your eyes that you might see, could you then see the spirits? Yes, as plainly as you now see bodies.[52]

Elder Parley P. Pratt, a modern-day apostle of the Lord Jesus Christ, also spoke of the nearness of the spirit world. He explained:

> As to its location, it is here on the very planet where we were born; or, in other words, the earth and other planets of a like sphere, have their inward or spiritual spheres, as well as their outward, or temporal. The one is peopled by temporal tabernacles, and the other by spirits. A veil is drawn between the one sphere and the other, whereby all the objects in the spiritual sphere are rendered invisible to those in the temporal.[53]

President Brigham Young taught the same principle as Elder Pratt and President Joseph F. Smith concerning the shared locations of Earth and the spirit world. He stated:

> Where is the spirit world? It is right here. . . .
> Do they go to the sun? No. Do they go beyond the boundaries of this organized earth? No, they do not.
> They are brought forth upon this earth, for the express purpose of inhabiting it to all eternity. Where else are you going? Nowhere else, only as you may be permitted.[54]

Elder Parley P. Pratt also spoke of the different locations within the spirit realm where the wicked and the righteous dwell and perform their activities:

> Many spirits of the departed, who are unhappy, linger in lonely wretchedness about the Earth, and in the air, and especially about their ancient homesteads, and the places rendered dear to them by the memory of the former scenes.[55]

But the nearness of the spirit realm does not render it visible to mortals. We cannot see their fine, less-physical, spirit bodies. So it is necessary for the Lord, or the Spirit of the Holy Ghost, to touch our eyes, or in some way move upon us, for us to be able to see the spirits in the next realm. Our coarse, less-refined mortal eyes cannot see such fine, pure matter as that of which spirits are made. A non-exact, but illustrative example might be the difference in hearing ability between a human and a dog. If one blows on a dog whistle, the human ear cannot even make it out. In fact, unless he sees the person blowing on the whistle, a human would be totally oblivious to the fact that there were any unheard sounds passing by his ears! But the dog down the street, or even right next to him, will be howling because of the agitating effects of the piercingly high frequency sound on its more refined, finer eardrums.

Why can we not see spirits, if they are all around us? Brigham Young answers:

> Spirits are just as familiar with spirits as bodies are with bodies, though spirits are composed of matter so refined as not to be tangible to this coarser organization [our mortal body and eyes]. They walk, converse, and have their meetings . . .[56]

Joseph Smith also explains:

> In tracing the thing to the foundation, and looking at it philosophically, we shall find a very material difference between the body and the spirit; the body is supposed to be organized matter, and the spirit, by many, is thought to be immaterial, without substance. With this latter statement we should beg leave to differ, and state the spirit is a substance; that it is material, but that it is more pure, elastic and refined matter than the body; that it existed before the body, can exist in the body; and will exist separate from the body, when the body will be moldering in the dust; and will in the resurrection, be again united with it.[57]

One of the ways this new place could be described is a place where we, as spirit beings with finer, spiritual material, can exist. No longer carrying the heavier and denser material of our physical bodies, we can pass through and around other heavier, denser, "mortal" things with little or no restriction—save only the restriction imposed by the type of people we have been. I mean that those spirits who, through repentance, were found to be pure and obedient, have far greater freedom of vision, action, access and movement (as well as other things) than the disobedient. All spirits are capable of movement, in varying degrees, again according to their level of righteousness and the freedoms or restrictions they have as to where their respective level of righteousness or wickedness allows them to go. Much more of this will be discussed in greater detail in later chapters.

Spirits, particularly those in spirit prison, will be restricted as to the places they may go. Subject to that sort of restriction, all spirits still retain their agency to choose the activities within the permitted areas and range of activities allowed for those of their level of righteousness.

Some people can complain that having such restrictions amounts to an absence of real agency. Those who do are misguided— they do not understand. In every part of existence, even on Earth, we have restrictions. Just because we choose to go into the White House or the Kremlin, we cannot do so. We cannot choose to flap our arms and fly as do birds, or swim to the depths of the ocean, unrestricted, as can fishes. Nor can we say, "I choose to be on Mars right now." We can say it, but doing so will not make it happen.

Perhaps the best illustration would be something closer to the restrictions that come upon us by virtue of our own prior actions. If one has become addicted to smoking, he cannot simply say, "I now choose to not have any such addiction—or the cravings and misery associated with it." Again, he can say it, but it will not automatically happen according to his latest "choice." The fact is, that addict did have his agency concerning the matter of addiction to smoking. But he exercised his agency some time ago, and chose to begin smoking. That choice brought with it certain baggage—an addiction to the substance he had chosen to smoke. Now, that earlier choice and the resulting restrictive addiction limit the further exercise of his agency. It is not that he never had full agency as to this choice. It is that the improper use of one's agency, by itself, brings about subsequent restrictions to his agency. Inaccurately, today's world teaches us that we are not accountable for our actions and that each person should get as much as everyone else, whether or not he has worked as hard to "deserve" it.

This is really only one of Satan's lying deceptions rampant in the world today. There are many others equally deceptive and designed to thwart our progress and acquisition of truth.

So will it be in the spirit world. For the most part, restrictions we have there will be the direct result of the self-imposed consequences of our use of agency—our choices—in both the pre-existence and especially in mortality. Those who feel we are being unfairly restricted, whether here on Earth, or in the spirit world, can usually look in the mirror to see the responsible person.

Those who have been righteous, keeping the basic commandments and receiving their sacred ordinances shall have greater opportunity given them to see mortals still on Earth. The very righteous will even have much, and maybe even all, of the memory of their pre-existence restored.

Those who are still struggling to obtain a testimony of Christ, will not be able to see as much, because they still have much work to do on their faith, repentance, indeed, on their personal worthiness of such greater privileges.

Let us return to additional aspects of this place that awaits us all. It is a vast place, even overwhelming to a new entrant, which we all will be at the beginning of our life after mortal death.

The word "death" is not used there, nor is there the fear that we here associate with mortal death—the passing from mortality to the next world. There we will find another expression used to identify this transition from mortality, one that conveys the impression of being a "new birth."

Those who have passed through mortal death understand that they are actually still alive. Only their mortal bodies are dead— temporarily—for in the resurrection, those bodies will be renewed and made immortal. For now, their spirits continue their life—in a different sphere—a spiritual sphere.

CHAPTER 11

THE SPIRIT WORLD

EXTERNAL CONDITIONS AND SURROUNDINGS

In the spirit world, spirits are unaffected by the heat and cold of the mortal Earth. There is, in fact, no concern about any of the various climates or weather. There is no inclement weather in the spirit world. No one will feel chilly or miserably hot. Everyone there will feel comfortable as to temperature and humidity. The spirit world, although existing on and around the Earth, is a separate "spirit" realm, and is, therefore, not actually a part of the "physical" realm of mortal Earth. In other words, a "spirit" climate, separate from the "physical" climate, exists there. In a later chapter, I retell part of the account of a doctor who temporarily passed from mortality into the spirit world during an extremely cold winter on Earth. In his entire account, he never mentions feeling any cold around him in his "spirit" involvement with the mortal realm.[58]

No one will be ill. There will be no pains, aches or injuries. There will be no crippled, deformed, deaf or blind spirits. All of the spirit beings there will be whole. No one will be physically infirm in any way. There will be no physical sickness whatsoever. The only sickness, if one would call it a sickness, will be the "spiritual sickness" of those who have lived a life of wickedness or evil while on Earth.

There will be no language barriers in the spirit world. Whatever the language people spoke on Earth, everyone will understand each other. Spirits there will communicate easily with each other.

In speaking of the sociality or inter-relationships in the spirit world, the prophet Joseph Smith taught that the post-mortal spirit world is an actual place where spirits reside and "where they converse together the same as we do on the Earth."[59]

The Doctrine and Covenants also teaches of such social relationships: "And that same sociality which exists among us here will exist among us there, coupled with eternal glory."[60]

Where the righteous dwell, order will prevail. Where the Spirit prevails, there is perfect order. Where the wicked and perverse dwell, (because of the continuing principle of agency) there may be activities that are not so orderly. But even the evil and perverse exercise of agency will be limited and restricted as to the areas in which such is allowed, and the spirit beings who can be affected by the low-dwelling purveyors thereof. Such will be the order of things.

One of the wonderful results of the order that clearly will prevail in a realm governed by God, is the ability of each individual spirit there to pursue his own activities of choice, within the realm or area to which he is entitled to live and move. We will be free from the outside world's events or catastrophes, and from the interference of more evil spirits. That is, no war, disease, earthquake, hurricane, or other natural or man-made problems will require an individual to interrupt his pursuit of proper and important endeavors.

There will not be general upward mobility of association. That is, a wicked individual who dwells in a lower level of the spirit world will not be able to travel to a higher level and associate with or hassle individuals who dwell there. There will be lateral or horizontal association, or the ability to associate with other individuals on the same level as one another. There will be the ability of those from a higher level to go, as they are assigned, to teach others in the same or lower level than they. But then, after doing so, each such higher-level minister or teacher will return to his attained, higher level. No one at any level will be allowed to harm any other spirit.

There are not small spirits—small children—as we would call them here. Remember, the spirits of everyone of us are adults. The spirit of a newborn on Earth is a full-grown spirit, having passed through some extended period of life in the pre-existence. This mature spirit is simply housed temporarily in an infant body when born into mortality, then in a small child's body and, eventually, in a full-grown mortal body as that individual grows older on Earth.

Some spirits on Earth are more mature—in character—than others. Some are definitely less mature in their character and personality, partly as a result of the immaturity and foolishness of their choices in the pre-existence and then on Earth. It may be partly because they have not yet had the opportunity to learn the great truths possible for them to learn on Earth or in the spirit world. Another reason for spiritual and emotional immaturity will be the choices certain spirits made while in the pre-existence and on Earth, to refuse to learn such truths and to apply them in their lives. Some will simply have refused to grow up emotionally and spiritually. They will not automatically do so upon entering the spirit world. Only sincere effort on the part of each individual will bring true spiritual growth and maturity.

We will recognize people we knew on Earth. Our association with family, loved ones and dear friends will be joyous and important. There, we will love just as intensely—perhaps much more—those people who were so important and dear to us on the Earth before our death. This greater sense of love will exist because of our realization of the importance of these family members and friends due to their being away from us, as well as, due to the absence of restrictions brought on by the limitations of our mortal bodies.

Many will have left mortality long before we did and we will have missed our association with them for years. Others are among those we left behind on Earth when we passed through the veil into the spirit world. We will still care immensely for them and be concerned for their welfare while we are away from them.

Much more will be said about the surroundings of the righteous in the world of spirits in the chapter that deals with the activities and nature of the righteous spirits in paradise. This is where we will "view" the place where we truly will want to find ourselves.

CHAPTER 12

THE SPIRIT WORLD

OUR CHARACTER AND DISPOSITION; FAITH STILL REQUIRED

Spirits in the spirit world will find themselves in one of a number of vastly contrasting circumstances. The differences in the places spirits are placed will be dependent upon the types of lives they lived on Earth and the progress they made while in mortality. In the spirit world, the great dividers will be: (1) The level of our goodness and obedience (how close to being like God we have become); and

(2) The receipt and acceptance of Christ's commandments and covenants. Those having excelled in both categories go to paradise.

I quote again what President Joseph F. Smith taught about the state of the souls of men after this life:

> The spirits of all men, as soon as they depart from this mortal body, whether they are good or evil, . . . are taken home to that God who gave them life, where there is a separation, a partial judgment, and the spirits of those who are righteous are received into a state of happiness which is called paradise, a state of rest, a state of peace, where they expand in wisdom, where they have respite from all their troubles, and where care and sorrow do not annoy. The wicked, on the contrary, have no part nor portion in the Spirit of the Lord, and they are cast into outer darkness, being led captive, because of their own iniquity, by the evil one. And in this space between death and the resurrection of the body, the two classes of souls remain, in happiness or in misery, until the time which is appointed of God that the dead shall come forth and be reunited both spirit and body, and be brought to stand before God, and be judged according to their works. This is the final judgment.[61]

Elder Bruce R. McConkie also explained:

> Until the death of Christ these two spirit abodes [paradise and hell] were separated by a great gulf, with the intermingling of their respective inhabitants strictly forbidden (Luke 16:19-31). After our Lord bridged the gulf between the two (1 Pet. 3:18-21; Moses 7:37-39), the affairs of his kingdom in the spirit world were so arranged that righteous spirits began teaching the gospel to wicked ones.[62]

Those individuals who on Earth did not achieve those two great dividing requirements are in the different parts of spirit prison:

(1) The good and honorable who are in a happy, but not completed spiritual position; (2) The less committed good are in a lesser, though relatively high level of spirit prison; and (3) Those who have rejected and even fought against the Savior and his anointed, who have voluntarily subjected themselves to Satan, are in a miserable place. They still pursue their earlier evil designs but are frustrated in that they are incapable of accomplishing them. The spirits in one of these different districts of spirit prison do not intermingle with spirits in the other districts or divisions. There may be more categories within these general levels, but these will suffice as to the basic divisions.

The prophet Alma gave this explanation:

> For behold, this life is the time for men to prepare to meet God; yea, behold the day of this life is the day for men to perform their labors.
>
> And now, as I said unto you before, as ye have had so many witnesses, therefore, I beseech of you that ye do not procrastinate the day of your repentance until the end; for after this day of life, which is given us to prepare for eternity, behold, if we do not improve our time while in this life, then cometh the night of darkness wherein there can be no labor performed.
>
> Ye cannot say, when ye are brought to that awful crisis, that I will repent, that I will return to my God. Nay, ye cannot say this; for that same spirit which doth possess your bodies at the time that ye go out of this life, that same spirit will have power to possess your body in that eternal world.[63]

As Alma states above, "that same spirit will have power to possess your body in that eternal world," the exact same spirit—or character and disposition—that exists within each of us as we leave our mortal life, remains in us as we enter the world to come, the world of spirits. We may say this in other words. We will be on the other side of the veil as we first enter the spirit world, exactly the same person, with exactly the same desires, appetites, intentions, wants, aspirations, character, dispositions and moods that we had just moments before as we dwelled in our last hours and minutes on Earth.

As quoted above, President Brigham Young said:

> Suppose, then, that a man is evil in his heart—wholly given up to wickedness, and in that condition dies, his spirit will enter into the spirit world intent upon evil.
>
> On the other hand, if we are striving with all the powers and faculties God has given us to improve upon our talents, to prepare ourselves to dwell in eternal life, and the grave receives our bodies while we are thus engaged, with what disposition will our spirits enter their next state? They will be still striving to do the things of God, only in a much greater degree—learning, increasing, growing in grace and in the knowledge of the truth.[64]

Upon entering the spirit world, one does not automatically become different in one's thoughts, likes, dislikes, desires, propensities, willingness to listen, unwillingness to listen, faith, interest in spiritual and religious matters, interest in studying (whether it be horticulture, mechanics, philosophy, astronomy, etc.)

In other words, if one has no interest in studying religion while on Earth, he will begin his existence in the spirit world still having no interest in doing so in the spirit realm. One, who on Earth had no inclination whatsoever to assist others in their needs, will feel just as unwilling in the world of spirits. One who refused to pursue eternal growth will, at least initially, still feel to refuse to do so.

The relative conditions and state of mind in the two spheres of the post-mortal spirit world are described by the prophet Joseph Smith. He revealed this about those who have not applied themselves in obeying God's commandments and in developing their character and faithfulness:

The great misery of departed spirits in the world of spirits, where they go after death, is to know that they come short of the glory that others enjoy and that they might have enjoyed themselves, and they are their own accusers.[65]

Of those who were righteous on Earth, he said:

The spirits of the just are exalted to a greater and more glorious work; hence they are blessed in their departure to the world of spirits. Enveloped in flaming fire, they are not far from us, and know and understand our thoughts, feelings, and motions, and are often pained therewith.[66]

Our Father will still insure our moral agency, our right to choose, even if we exercise it to our own detriment. He will insure that we are not pushed to accept exalting truths or to choose happiness. If we choose to remain ignorant of those truths that can make us forever happy, God will not force our will. That was, after all, Lucifer's rejected plan. Our ability to choose for ourselves is the very thing necessary for us to get from here to eternal life—our agency to choose to exercise faith in the Lord Jesus Christ in doing things necessary to become like He is. Lucifer's plan is nothing more than a vicious and lying hoax that he perpetrated upon a third part of the host of heaven in the pre-existence and that he continues to perpetrate upon the souls of men, women and children on Earth. Those who followed Satan on Earth will retain the same nature and disposition to choose and to do evil in the spirit world.

Why will God not require us to at least listen to something true that is for our good? There are at least two reasons: (1) it is by the exercise of faith that we progress. One of those eternal laws that God obeys is the necessity of our having the complete right to make our own choices, whether for good and truth, or for evil and lies. He

51

allows us to choose, whether one's choice is for eternal progress and happiness, or for eternal damnation and misery; and (2) He is God because He has in the past obeyed, and will always obey eternal laws and truths.

The words to the religious hymn "Know This, That Every Soul Is Free" address this well:

> Know this, that every soul is free to choose his life and what he'll be; For this eternal truth is giv'n: That God will force no man to heav'n.
>
> He'll call, persuade, direct aright, and bless with wisdom, love, and light, in nameless ways be good and kind, but never force the human mind.
>
> Freedom and reason make us men; take these away, what are we then? Mere animals, and just as well. The beasts may think of heav'n or hell.
>
> May we no more our pow'rs abuse, but ways of truth and goodness choose; Our God is pleased when we improve His grace and seek His perfect love.[67]

The war in heaven was fought in good part in order for God, our Father, to preserve and guarantee the continuation and blessings of our eternal agency. The right to exercise our moral agency to choose right or wrong is absolutely necessary for each of us to become like God our Father. Without temptation and the opportunity and right to choose evil, one cannot show his faithfulness and obedience in choosing to do good. Satan fought to take away from us that moral agency, our right to choose which way we would go. He still continues his evil and selfish battle against us and against our moral agency.

Because He loves us, God our Father wants us to choose to learn, accept, progress and become all that we may become—all that He is. For that reason, He introduced and put into effect His great plan of salvation—for our eternal good and happiness.

Why does an earthly father take his children on vacations where he has already traveled? Why does he support them in receiving a college education or provide any number of other benefits to his children? It costs him in time, planning, money, headaches and sometimes even heartache, to provide those things for them. What does he receive for his efforts and sacrifice? The biggest reward for that earthly father is the joy of seeing his children experience new and exciting places and things, learn from these experiences and improve themselves so they can someday provide a good life for themselves and for their own families.

God, our Father, has far greater love, knowledge and vision than any earthly father. He provided our travel to Earth, allowing us to experience new and different things. He allowed us to receive our bodies, experience growth-providing opportunities and challenges, to learn worldly things and to understand and receive soul-saving principles and ordinances.

A high-quality college education with effort expended by the student to learn and excel—not just enough to pass the classes—will generally allow that graduated student to earn more than otherwise and to live a more fulfilled and enjoyable life. So will a quality education in mortality—with efforts expended by the student-of-mortality to learn and excel in God like endeavors—insure that this Earth-graduate will earn more eternal rewards than otherwise could ever be possible. This allows the individual to live for the rest of forever—eternity—a more fulfilled, even God-like, life.

All of our choices—assured to us by our God-given agency—require the exercise of faith. Without faith in the Lord Jesus Christ, we lack the essential requirement to fully progress spiritually. Faith in the earthly education system can be the motivating factor in our expending time and money at a university to learn and prepare ourselves for an earthly occupation. Faith in Christ is even more the necessary first ingredient for anyone to accept eternal truths and eternal life-saving, or eternal life-bringing, qualities to our characters and dispositions.

Ultimately, one's goodness and obedience to God's commandments will determine where he will find himself hereafter. It is useful for one to have learned much about many types of things. But one subject stands supreme in importance to each spirit child of God—the study of God-like knowledge and attributes.

The following analogy is instructive.

If one is attending medical school to become a doctor, it is nice for him to have learned about astronomy and horticulture, literature and history. Those subjects have their interest and can help give a person breadth of understanding. But if that medical student does not pass his medical school exams, he may be quite well-rounded, but he will not be a doctor. Also, if he does not learn well what he needed to study in medical school, including the practical how-to's of functioning as a doctor, he will make a poor doctor.

Likewise, studying horticulture, literature, history—even medicine—on Earth will have its benefits to a graduate of mortality. But those subjects, even the supposed mastery of them, will not qualify anyone to return to the presence of God or to become like He is. Only the study and sincere application of the Lord's true gospel principles, covenants and ordinances will bring anyone to dwell forever with God—having become greater and more glorious than anyone can become by any other means.

How do we obtain great knowledge of eternal and earthly subjects? What is the best way to obtain it? The Lord answers that question in His revelation found in The Doctrine and Covenants, Section 93: "He that keepeth his commandments receiveth truth and light, until he is glorified in truth and knoweth all things."[68]

We learn from that verse that the way for each of us to learn every type of truth, spiritual and temporal, is to keep the commandments of God. Doing so allows us to have the presence and assistance of the Holy Ghost.

Moroni teaches us the same principle: "And by the power of the Holy Ghost, ye may know the truth of all things."[69]

Having the presence and assistance of the Holy Ghost expands our minds and our mental abilities and capacities. Therefore, our learning capacity is greatly enhanced by Its presence and assistance.

Let me illustrate this principle through the use of mortal comparisons. One who merely hears something—through his sense of hearing—does not learn or remember a concept as well as one who both hears and sees that same concept—using both the sense of hearing and the sense of sight. In a similar way, one who seeks knowledge and learning through his normal mortal senses and mental faculties will not—cannot—learn or retain nearly as much as one who uses the same level of mortal senses and mental faculties, enhanced by the mind-expanding ability of this third member of the Godhead, the Holy Ghost.

As we will learn in later chapters, the abilities and capacities of our spirit are substantially greater when not restricted by the physical limitations of our mortal body. In at least one sense, those greater abilities and capacities are "freed" from some of our physical limitations of mortality when we allow—through obedience and faithfulness—the Spirit to "open" our minds to greater receptivity and understanding.

Furthermore, what God and His Spirit know and understand are infinitely more and greater than what we know and understand. So what the Spirit can teach us is well beyond what we may ever discover on our own.

CHAPTER 13

THE SPIRIT WORLD

ASSOCIATIONS WE CAN HAVE AND HOW NATURAL WE WILL FEEL THERE

What about Satan and his wicked followers who gave us such a difficult time while we were on the Earth? What power or influence will they have over us in the spirit world if we were striving earnestly to be obedient and faithful while on the Earth? What influence or control over us will they have in the spirit world?

President Brigham Young taught that the righteous will be free from any influence, power or harm from the wicked in the spirit world:

> If we are faithful to our [true, restored] religion,
> when we go into the spirit world, the fallen spirits–Lucifer
> and the third part of the heavenly hosts that came with

him, and the spirits of wicked men who have dwelt upon this earth, the whole of them combined will have no influence over our spirits. Is not that an advantage? Yes. All the rest of the children of men are more or less subject to them, and they are subject to them as they were while here in the flesh.[70]

He further explained:

The faithful and true followers of Christ, who have received the Priesthood, will have power over all of the evil spirits, even those who may have had power or authority over them in mortality, for they have overcome them. Those evil spirits are under the command and control of every man that has had the Priesthood on him, and has honored it in the flesh, just as much as my hand is under my control.[71]

What types of associations, if any, will exist in the spirit world? Comparatively, the length of our pre-existence is abundantly greater than the length of time we spend on Earth—the bulk of which time is spent growing up, pursuing selfish endeavors and providing for ourselves and our families. Therefore, we would certainly have had the opportunity to get to know and love many more people during our pre-mortal existence than we have been able to do on Earth. We can expect to know and enjoy being around many more spirits in the post-mortal realm than was possible for us on Earth.

We will find more acquaintances—family members and even close and beloved friends—in the spirit world than we have had on Earth. Our joy in mingling with them will be greater than it could ever be while in mortality.

LeRoi C. Snow temporarily passed into the spirit world. He related his experience there. He had a great desire to get there. Once there, he immediately recognized an absence of cares and worries. He also spoke of meeting many people he knew.

> As soon as I had a glimpse of the other world I
> was anxious to go and all the care and worry left me.
> I entered a large hall. It was so long that I
> could not see the end of it. It was filled with people. . . .
> I passed on through the room and met a great
> many of my relatives and friends. It was like going along
> the crowded streets of a city where you meet many
> people, only a very few of whom you recognize . . .
> Everybody appeared to be perfectly happy. I was
> having a very pleasant visit with each one that I knew. . . .[72]

Will it seem strange to be in such a place? Will we feel out-of-place there? No. Things there will seem very normal and natural to us. Our spirits will be very much "at home" in that spirit realm, for we will be among those who have also been striving to live as they should while on the Earth.

Peter Johnson, a latter-day missionary, became ill with malaria and went into the spirit realm for more than an hour in September 1898. He wrote of his experience there:

> My spirit left the body: just how I cannot tell. But
> I perceived myself standing some four or five feet in the
> air, and saw my body lying on the bed. I felt perfectly
> natural, but as this was a new condition, I began to make
> observations. I turned my head, shrugged my shoulders,
> felt with my hands, and realized that it was myself. I also
> knew that my body was lying, lifeless, on the bed. While I
> was in the new environment, it did not seem strange, for
> I realized everything that was going on, and perceived that
> I was the same in the spirit as I had been in the body.[73]

Lorenzo Dow Young, a brother of Brigham Young, saw in vision the process of death, the spirit world and the celestial kingdom. He told of both how natural it felt being there in the spirit world and of the nearness of departed ones to those they love on Earth. He wrote:

> I had a remarkable dream or vision. I fancied that I died. In a moment I was out of the body, and fully conscious that I had made the change. At once, a heavenly messenger, or guide, was by me. I thought and acted as naturally as I had done in the body, and all my sensations seemed as complete without as with it. . . . [74]

For the righteous, passage from mortality to the spirit world is easy and natural. This travel and change will take place almost without our notice. That is, there was little perceptible difference in how the individuals felt before and after they had passed from mortal Earth to the spirit world. Obviously, had the individual been in great pain just before the change, there would be a recognition of an immediate cessation of all such pain. That realization would then be followed by a sensing of one's being in a different realm or department of the world—the spirit portion.

CHAPTER 14

THE SPIRIT WORLD

OUR INCREASED CAPABILITIES

As the quotations in this chapter will teach, to the righteous in the spirit realm, the beauty, the brightness and the wonder of this next stop in eternity will be amazing. We will not stumble or fall. We will not scratch, cut or hurt ourselves. The faithful will find themselves able to move with ease, and at incredible speed! Note that most of the increased capabilities in the spirit world are experienced by the righteous and obedient beings who pass there from mortality. The wicked also have certain of the increase in abilities, but theirs will be far fewer in number and lesser in extent than will be those granted to righteous spirits.

In his vision of the spirit world, Lorenzo Dow Young noticed the beauty of that realm and was reluctant to leave it. He recorded:

> I could distinctly see the world from which we had
> first come. . . . To me, it looked cloudy, dreary and dark.
> I was filled with sad disappointment, I might say horror,
> at the idea of returning there. I supposed I had come to
> stay in that heavenly place, which I had so long desired to

see; up to this time, the thought had not occurred to me that I would be required to return.

I plead with my guide to let me remain. He replied that I was permitted to only visit the heavenly cities, for I had not filled my mission in yonder world; therefore I must return and take my body. . .

We returned to my house. There I found my body, and it appeared to me dressed for burial. It was with great reluctance that I took possession of it to resume the ordinary avocations of life, and endeavor to fill the important mission I had received. I awoke and found myself in my bed. I lay and meditated the remainder of the night on what had been shown me.[75]

The cloudy and dark appearance of the Earth may be explained in part by the vision of the prophet Enoch, who

. . . [b]eheld Satan; and he had a great chain in his hand, and it veiled the whole face of the earth with darkness; and he looked up and laughed, and his angels rejoiced.[76]

The vision of spirits, or their ability to see, will be greatly enhanced, due to the lack of a mortal film or limitation on our eyes. Further explanation is found in I Corinthians 13:12. The Apostle Paul tells us "We see through a glass darkly." Perhaps we can in one sense only more easily understand the effects of mortality on our eyes by comparing our view of things around us on Earth, looking through a dirty window, compared to looking through a clear glass, or no glass at all. In fact, in Revelation 4:6 and 15:2, John describes the place where God and Christ dwell as being a "sea of glass" or a "crystal." That is quite a contrast to our clouded, dark, earthly views.

There is another, more significant reason for immensely improved vision in the world of spirits. Elder Orson Pratt, a modern-day apostle, taught that in some way we will be able to see things with our whole being. Rather than looking through two small, restricted lenses—our mortal eyes—we will be seeing with our entire self. That would be a multiplication of many, many times! This is part of the greatly increased powers and capabilities of righteous spirits.

In a later chapter, I will write of our vastly expanded mental capabilities.

As spirit beings in the world of spirits, we will once again have full, or at least fuller, use of the capabilities and powers we had in the pre-existence, which capabilities and powers became very restricted and diminished while we were on Earth, living in mortal bodies. Let's now refer to an extensive explanation from Elder Orson Pratt, who taught concerning these expanded abilities. He stated:

> Our happiness here is regulated in a great measure by external objects, by the organization of the mortal tabernacle; they are not permitted to rise very high, or to become very great; on the other hand it seems to be a kind of limit to our joys and pleasures, sufferings, and pains, and this is because of the imperfection of the tabernacle in which we dwell; and of those things with which we are surrounded; but in that life everything will appear in its true colors; . . . This tabernacle, although it is good in its place, is something like the scaffolding you see round about a new building that is going up; it is only a help, an aid in this imperfect situation; but when we get into another condition, we shall find that these imperfect aids will not be particularly wanted; we shall have other sources of gaining knowledge, besides these inlets, called senses.[77]

Elder Orson Pratt also taught that righteous spirits have the power to communicate by merely projecting their very thoughts. They need not actually speak them. Not only is this possible, but this method of communicating is faster and more precise than speaking. The individual to whom such communication is sent understands not only much, much better that which is communicated, it might be said that the receiving spirit thoroughly and accurately understands the full and precise meaning conveyed by the communicator. The breadth and range of words or concepts that can be communicated far exceed that of any earthly language. As I have experienced in writing this book, and as we all have experienced in attempting to explain some feeling, ailment or desire, we bump up against the limits of our language. We simply cannot express in English—nor in any other earthly language—all we can sense, desire, dream or imagine. Apparently, there are not such restrictions or limitations in a righteous spirit's capability to communicate to another spirit in the spirit world. If one desires to communicate, it just occurs as he forms the thoughts of that desired conversation. The result is full understanding of the desired message.[78]

In addition to being able to see better and to communicate thoroughly, righteous spirits also shall have dramatically increased speed and capacity to move around. Not only is speed multiplied, a righteous spirit's ability to go great distances is also incredible.

In 1871, Brigham Young spoke at the funeral services of Miss Aurelia Spencer. He taught of both our present life and the spirit world. He explained:

> The brightness and glory of the next apartment is inexpressible. It is not encumbered with this clog of dirt we are carrying around here so that when we advance in years we have to be stubbing along and to be careful lest we fall down. We see our youth, even, frequently stubbing their toes and falling down. But yonder, how different! They move with ease and like lightning. If we want to visit Jerusalem, or this, that, or the other place—and I presume we will be permitted if we desire—there we are, looking at its streets. . . . If we wish to understand how they are living here on these western islands, or in China, we are there; in fact, we are like the light of the morning, . . .[79]

At the funeral of President Daniel Spencer in 1868, he taught concerning the same principle:

> As quickly as the spirit is unlocked from this house
> of clay, it is free to travel with lightning speed to any
> planet, or fixed star, or to the uttermost part of the earth,
> or to the depths of the sea, according to the will of Him
> who dictates.[80]

Similar powers of locomotion were seen in the actions of the young boy, Briant Stevens, who appeared to his father in a dream the night after he had died of tetanus, on February 3, 1887. Another man writes of the father's experience:

> At length he saw a light and in this light was little
> Briant, standing in the air, robed in snowy whiteness,
> with a face transfigured in its light and beauty. The boy
> smiled at him and moved his hands as if in loving
> recognition. This ethereal form of Briant moved about
> in the room without effort. A single inclination of the
> shining head seemed to project the body in any desired
> direction.[81]

President Joseph F. Smith spoke of the expanded ability to move around that spirit beings enjoy. He said:

> The disembodied spirit during the interval of the
> death of the body and its resurrection from the grave is
> not perfect, hence it is not prepared to enter into the
> exaltation of the celestial kingdom; but it has the privilege
> of soaring in the midst of immortal beings, and of enjoying
> to a certain extent, the presence of God, not the fulness
> of his glory, not the fulness of the reward which we are
> seeking and which we are destined to receive, if found

faithful to the law of the celestial kingdom, but only in part.[82]

Even the ability to travel through time seems to be available to the righteous spirits. Brigham Young explained it this way:

> If we want to behold Jerusalem as it was in the days of the Savior; or if we want to see the Garden of Eden as it was when created, there we are; and we see it as it existed spiritually, for it was created first spiritually and then temporally, and spiritually it still remains. And when there we may behold the earth as at the dawn of creation, or we may visit any city we please that exists upon its surface.[83]

The apostle Elder Orson Pratt also explained:

> When I speak of the future state of man, and the situation of our spirits between death and the resurrection, I long for the experience and knowledge to be gained in that state, as well as this. We shall learn many more things there; we need not suppose our five senses connect us with all the things of heaven, and earth, and eternity, and space; we need not think that we are conversant with all the elements of nature, through the medium of the senses God has given us here. Suppose He should give us a sixth sense, a seventh, an eighth, a ninth, or a fiftieth. All these different senses would convey to us new ideas, as much so as the senses of tasting, smelling, or seeing communicate different ideas from that of hearing.
>
> Do we suppose the five senses of man converse with all the elements of nature? No. There is a principle called magnetism; we see its effects, but the name of the thing does not give us a knowledge of its nature, or of the manner

in which the effects are produced. We know not why a piece of iron will turn towards a magnet this way or that. Now, suppose we had a sixth sense that was so adapted as to perceive this very thing, we should learn some new ideas, connected with the elements of nature, besides those we have learned by the five senses we already possess. I believe there are ten thousand things with which we are surrounded, that we know nothing about by our present natural senses. When the Lord imparts to us a principle by which we can look upon the past and future, as well as the present—by which we can look upon many intricate objects of nature which are now hidden from our view, we shall find our capacity for obtaining and retaining knowledge to be greatly enlarged.

We already have the capacity, and all it wants is to bring things into a situation to act upon it. The capacity is here; and when the Lord sees fit, it will be instructed and taught, and things will be unveiled—even the things of God, and the laws that have been hidden concerning the celestial, terrestrial, and telestial worlds, and concerning all the variety of things that are organized in the immensity of space, so far as the Lord sees proper to unfold them; and we shall learn more and more of them until the . . . Lord places us in circumstances to become acquainted with them.[84]

As we have previously mentioned, our capacity to see will be magnificently expanded, for our eyes will not clouded. Moreover, our eyes will not be the only parts of our being that will receive and process light. Consider only the effect of having exceptionally clear, unfettered eyes, and then magnify that by expanding those optics to encompass our entire bodies!

Elder Pratt continued his explanation:

We become acquainted with light and color through the organization of our bodies.

In other words the Lord has constructed the mortal eye and framed it in such a manner that it is capable of being acted upon by one of the elements of nature, called light; and that gives us a great variety of knowledge . . .

Suppose that the whole spirit were uncovered and exposed to all the rays of light, can it be supposed that light would not affect the spirit if it were thus unshielded, uncovered, and unclothed?

Do you suppose that it would not be susceptible of any impressions made by the elements of light? The spirit is inherently capable of experiencing the sensations of light; if it were not so, we could not see. You might form as fine an eye as ever was made, but if the spirit, in and of itself, were not capable of being acted upon by the rays of light, an eye would be of no benefit. Then unclothe the spirit, and instead of exposing a small portion of it about the size of a pea to the action of the rays of light, the whole of it would be exposed. I think we could then see in different directions at once, instead of looking in one particular direction, we could then look all around us at the same instant. . . . Then there would be a vast field opened to the view of the spirit, and this would be opened not in one direction only, but in all directions; . . . when this tabernacle is taken off; we shall look, not in one direction only, but in every direction. This will be calculated to give us new ideas, concerning the immensity of the creations of God, concerning worlds that may be far beyond the reach of the most powerful instruments that have been called to the aid of man. This will give us information and knowledge we never can know as long as we dwell in this mortal tabernacle.[85]

President Heber C. Kimball also spoke of the vision he had received of the greatly increased power of sight in spirit beings:

> All at once my vision was opened, and the walls
> of the building were no obstruction to my seeing, for I
> saw nothing but the visions that presented themselves.
> Why did not the walls obstruct my view? Because my
> spirit could look through the walls of that house, for I
> looked with that spirit, element, and power, with which
> angels look; and as God sees all things, so were
> invisible things brought before me, as the Lord would
> bring things before Joseph in the Urim and Thummim.
> It was upon that principle that the Lord showed things
> to the prophet Joseph.[86]

As previously quoted, there are likely to be multiple other senses—in addition to our current five (which five will have even been enhanced)—that we may enjoy in the spirit world. Because the following quotation addresses the current topic as well as the previous one, I choose to repeat what Elder Orson Pratt said of these additional senses:

> When I speak of the future state of man, and the
> situation of our spirits between death and the resurrection,
> I long for the experience and knowledge to be gained in
> that state, as well as this. We shall learn many more things
> there; we need not suppose our five senses connect us
> with all the things of heaven, and earth, and eternity, and
> space; we need not think that we are conversant with all
> the elements of nature, through the medium of the senses

God has given us here. Suppose He should give us a sixth sense, a seventh, an eighth, a ninth, or a fiftieth. All these different senses would convey to us new ideas, as much so as the senses of tasting, smelling, or seeing communicate different ideas from that of hearing.[87]

In this discourse he went on to describe some of these senses and powers that are to be characteristic of spirit beings, and commented on three in particular.

First, he described the greatly increased ability to remember that is possessed by spirit beings.

We read or learn a thing by observation yesterday, and to-day (sic) or tomorrow it is gone, . . . some of the knowledge we receive here at one time becomes so completely obliterated, through the weakness of the animal system, that we cannot call it to mind, no association of ideas will again suggest it to our minds; it is gone, erased, eradicated from the tablet of our memories. This is not owing to the want of capacity in the spirit; no, but the spirit has a full capacity to remember . . . it is not the want of capacity in the spirit of man that causes him to forget the knowledge he may have learned yesterday; but it is because of the imperfection of the tabernacle in which the spirit dwells; because there is imperfection in the organization of the flesh and bones, and in things pertaining to the tabernacle; it is this that erases from our memory many things that would be useful; we cannot retain them in our minds, they are gone into oblivion. It is not so with the spirit when it is released from this tabernacle. . . . Wait until these mortal bodies are laid in the tomb; when we return home to God who gave us life; then is the time we shall have the most vivid knowledge of all the past acts of our lives during our probationary state.[88]

Even the ability to learn and ponder multiple, different ideas and concepts at one time will be part of our spirit capabilities. Elder Orson Pratt taught this principle:

> There is a faculty mentioned in the word of God, which we are not in possession of here, but we shall possess it hereafter; that is not only to see a vast number of things in the same moment, looking in all directions by the aid of the Spirit, but also to obtain a vast number of ideas at the same instant. . . . I believe we shall be freed, in the next world, in a great measure, from these narrow, contracted methods of thinking. Instead of thinking in one channel, and following up one certain course of reasoning to find a certain truth, knowledge will rush in from all quarters; it will come in like the light which flows from the sun, penetrating every part, informing the spirit, and giving understanding concerning ten thousand things at the same time; and the mind will be capable of receiving and retaining all. . . .
>
> Here, then, is a new faculty of knowledge, very extended in its nature, that is calculated to throw a vast amount of information upon the mind of man, almost in the twinkling of an eye. How long a time would it take a man in the next world, if he had to gain knowledge as we do here, to find out the simplest things in nature? He might reason, and reason for thousands of years, and then would have hardly gotten started. But when this Spirit of God, this great telescope that is used in the celestial heavens, is given to man, and he, through the aid of it, gazes upon eternal things, what does he behold? Not one object at a time, but a vast multitude of objects rush before his vision, and are present before his mind, filling him in a moment with the knowledge of worlds more numerous than the sands of the sea shore. Will he be able to bear it? Yes, his mind is strengthened in

proportion to the amount of information imparted.
It is this tabernacle, in its present condition, that
prevents us from a more enlarged understanding.[89]

So the righteous spirits in paradise will be able to learn from many, or all parts of their body, including through many senses beyond the mere five senses with which we can learn and experience things on Earth. Knowledge and light will be able to flow into a righteous spirit from every direction. Included in this learning will actually be the re-acquisition or recalling of knowledge once had in the pre-existence but withheld from mortals on the Earth. This knowledge is restored as the veil of mortality is lifted from the minds of righteous spirits in paradise.

Lawrence Tooley recalled a conversation he had with his spirit-world guide, a former earthly friend whose name was also Larry:

. . . I was acutely aware of everything around me.
I feel as if all my senses have increased a hundred fold.
. . . I was again in possession of superior knowledge
and intelligence . . . withheld from me since I had first
gone to earth.
[He was told:] "Since you've crossed over, the veil
has been taken from your mind. You'll soon regain all
your powers and knowledge. . . . . I'm talking about a
recall of your former knowledge and powers."[90]

Additional learning will be available to the righteous who desire knowledge of many different subjects. In the spirit world, the reader "experiences" the book. He does not merely read it. Thus, a righteous individual learns in a greater way. We all know that one learns best by experience, not just by hearing or reading about something. We can never fully "know" how searing a hot plate on a range really is, unless we touch it. Having experienced that very real "hot," we now understand—we have really learned—what that word and the concept of "hot" really mean. So if we can experience the words, the thoughts, the intentions and purposes, even the feelings of the author, we know much more than if we only read the words and phrases contained in the book itself. Since we will not experience pain, discomfort or injury in the spirit world, we will be able to "experience" all types of things without worry.

The prophet Joseph Smith taught the importance of knowledge, and therefore, learning. He said:

> A man is saved no faster than he gets knowledge, for if he does not get knowledge, he will be brought into captivity by some evil power in the other world, as evil spirits will have more knowledge, and consequently more power than many men who are on the earth.[91]

Lawrence (Larry) Tooley spoke of his experience of passing to the other side of the veil. His experience beyond the veil complements the prophet Joseph's teachings. Tooley's guide explained some of the reasons for the great interest in learning as he showed Larry a spirit-world learning center. The guide told him:

> ... Here everyone has a burning thirst for knowledge.
> One of our greatest joys here is the pursuit of knowledge. . . .
> ... knowledge increases our intelligence. The greater our field of knowledge and experience, the more intelligent we become. . . .
> ... If we're going to inherit Father's Kingdom, we need to be intelligent enough to administer in the affairs of the Kingdom.[92]

In the spirit world, we find that our ability to receive and process new information has expanded dramatically. Our mental capabilities are far greater than they were on Earth.

Lance Richardson's spirit left his body following a serious automobile accident. He recounted:

> I had a tremendous mental agility. My mind was so quick, and I was able to see in every direction at the same time.
>
> I realized later I was not seeing with my natural eyes. I was perceiving and comprehending everything around me.
>
> At the same time, I was feeling an enormous mental capacity.
>
> It was nothing new. I was aware that I had always been this way. It felt very natural.
>
> It was the real me. I didn't have to think about it. That was the natural way of things, and I felt very comfortable, very relaxed. . . .
>
> My ability to comprehend and learn had been multiplied a thousand times or more. The slow, clunky manner in which I learned on earth had evaporated. I could absorb and comprehend things I never thought possible.[93]

Knowledge and intelligence are tremendously important in not only the spirit world, but everywhere in God's plan. Let's review just a few of the scriptural passages that refer to the importance of knowledge and intelligence:

> "The glory of God is intelligence, or, in other words, light and truth."[94]

> "Truth is knowledge of things as they are, and as they were, and as they are to come."[95]

> For intelligence cleaveth unto intelligence; wisdom receiveth wisdom; truth embraceth truth; virtue loveth

virtue; light cleaveth unto light; mercy hath compassion on
mercy and claimeth her own; justice continueth its course
and claimed its own; judgment goeth before the face of him
who sitteth upon the throne and governeth and executeth
all things.

He comprehendeth all things, and all things are
before him, and all things are round about him; and he is
above all things, and in all things, and is through all things, and
is round about all things; and all things are by him, and of
him, even God, forever and ever.[96]

For the word of the Lord is truth, and whatsoever is
truth is light, and whatsoever is light is Spirit, even the spirit
of Jesus Christ.

And the Spirit giveth light to every man that cometh
into the world; and the Spirit enlighteneth every man
through the world, that hearkeneth to the voice of the
Spirit.[97]

The prophet Joseph Smith taught about the differences in the
level of intelligence of the spirit children of God that existed so very
long ago in the pre-existence. God, whose spirit was housed in His
immortal physical body, was pre-eminent among the spirits there. He
was more intelligent than not only any one of the other intelligences—
spirits—there. He was more intelligent than all of the others
combined![98]

We, as intelligent spirits, are co-eternal with God, our Father.
Joseph Smith taught:

God himself, finding he was in the midst of spirits
and glory, because he was more intelligent, saw proper to
institute laws whereby the rest could have a privilege to
advance like himself. The relationship we have with God
places us in a situation to advance in knowledge. He has
power to institute laws to instruct the weaker intelligences,

that they may be exalted with himself, so that they might
have one glory upon another, and all that knowledge,
power, glory, and intelligence, which is requisite in order
to save them in the world of spirits.[99]

The above quotation, by itself, helps answer the questions billions of people ask, "Where did we come from? Why are we here? Where are we going after this life?"

As we briefly stated in an earlier chapter where we reviewed God's great plan of salvation, the answers can be concisely given. We dwelled with God, our Father, in the pre-existence. Because of His great love for, and desire to bless us, He allowed us to each individually choose to come to Earth. We came here to receive a mortal body and to progress in our quest to return to dwell forever with God in an exalted state. After mortality, we proceed to the spirit world, where we may continue our progression. Thereafter, we will go to a kingdom of glory, based upon the level of obedience and perfection we have attained through those prior three realms of existence.

God's desire was that we be given the opportunity to advance—even be exalted—with Himself, that we might receive knowledge, power, glory and intelligence. This loving and all-knowing God proceeded to provide each of us the blessing of coming to this Earth. He created this Earth for the express purpose of enabling us to progress to the point that we could become even as He is. Essential to this process, He even provided a Savior who would suffer incredible pain and an ignominious death to ransom us from our sins if we will repent and follow His commandments.

As the righteous spirits progress and perfect the talents they had on Earth, they will be given additional talents in order for them to be able to continue to improve and perfect themselves. Remember, the purpose of each of the stages of our eternal existence, including the world of spirits, is for the spirit children of God our Father to further their progress in becoming like Him. As we progress from one talent

75

to another, from one grace to another, we are definitely proceeding in that direction. As we become more like God in one area of knowledge, then we are given the opportunity to choose to become more and more like Him in another area, and then another, and on and on until we can, if we are faithful and diligent, become fully as He is! That is our destiny, for we are His literal spirit children and heirs.

Children grow up to be like their parents in most ways. On Earth, a child of human parents will not grow up to be like the offspring of a horse, cow or elephant. The human child will become a man or woman. If that child diligently applies himself to learning and working, he will come to equal or even exceed the level of achievement his parents achieved. We are the spirit children of God our Father. Our God-desired destiny is to become like our heavenly parents—like God. There is a difference between man and his offspring's possibilities of achievement and God and his spirit offspring's possibilities. A mortal child may, through diligence and effort, exceed the level of accomplishment, knowledge and ability of his parent. The best a spirit child of God can ever hope to do, by his obedience and diligent efforts, is to achieve—through the atonement and grace of the Lord Jesus Christ—the same level of accomplishment, exaltation, that God, our Father, enjoys, except perhaps for the level of glory commensurate with the number of worlds and spirit children He has.

Of course, that will be enough. To have all knowledge, all power, and to have developed God's level of love and grace, will be glorious and beyond our current ability to even imagine.

CHAPTER 15

THE SPIRIT WORLD

LIMITATIONS IN SOME CAPABILITIES

Although there will be dramatically increased abilities restored to spirits, there will also be some limitations in the spirit world. One of the most significant limitations will be in our ability to repent and rid ourselves of sinful tendencies and dispositions. With that in mind, let us re-visit some verses from the Book of Alma we read in a prior chapter:

> For behold, this life is the time for men to prepare to meet God; yea, behold the day of this life is the day for men to perform their labors.
> And now, as I said unto you before, as ye have had so many witnesses, therefore, I beseech of you that ye do not procrastinate the day of your repentance until the end; for after this day of life, which is given us to prepare for eternity, behold, if we do not improve our time while in this life, then cometh the night of darkness wherein there can be no labor performed.

77

Ye cannot say, when ye are brought to that awful crisis, that I will repent, that I will return to my God. Nay, ye cannot say this; for that same spirit which doth possess your bodies at the time that ye go out of this life, that same spirit will have power to possess your body in that eternal world.[100]

Elder Melvin J. Ballard taught this important principle:

A man may receive the priesthood and all its privileges and blessings, but until he learns to overcome the flesh, his temper, his tongue, his disposition to indulge in the things God has forbidden, he cannot come into the Celestial Kingdom of God—until he overcomes either in this life or in the life to come. But this life is the time in which men are to repent.

Do not let any of us imagine that we can go down to the grave not having overcome the corruptions of the flesh and then lose in the grave all our sins and evil tendencies. They will be with us. They will be with the spirit when separated from the body.

I have said it is my judgment that any man or woman can do more to conform to the laws of God in one year in this life than they could in ten years when they are dead.

The spirit only can repent and change, and then the battle has to go forward with the flesh afterwards. It is much easier to overcome and serve the Lord when both flesh and spirit are combined as one. This is the time when men are more pliable and susceptible. We will find when we are dead every desire, every feeling will be greatly intensified. When clay is pliable it is much easier to change than when it gets hard and sets.

This life is the time to repent. That is why I presume it will take a thousand years after the first resurrection until the last group will be prepared to come forth. It will take them a thousand years to do what it would have taken, but three score years to accomplish in this life. And, so, we are to labor and have as little to do when we get through with this life as possible.

You remember the vision of the redemption of the dead as given to the Church through the late President Joseph F. Smith. President Smith saw the spirits of the righteous dead after their resurrection and the language is the same as one of the prophet Joseph's revelations–that they, the righteous dead, looked upon the absence of their spirits from their bodies as a bondage.

I grant you that the righteous dead will be at peace, but I tell you that when we go out of this life, leave this body, we will yearn to do a thousand things that we cannot do at all without the body, and how handicapped we will be, and realize then like a man who has suddenly lost both arms and his legs. We will be seriously handicapped, and we will long for the body; we will crave it; we will pray for that early reunion with our bodies. We will know then what advantage it was to have a body.

Then, every man and woman who is putting off until the next life the task of correcting and overcoming the weakness of the flesh are sentencing themselves to that many years of bondage, for no man or woman will come forth in the resurrection until they have completed their work, until they have overcome, until they have corrected, until they have done as much as they can do. That is why Jesus said in the resurrection there is neither marriage or giving in marriage, for all such contracts—agreements—will be provided for those who are worthy of it before men and women come forth in the resurrection of the Lord, and those who are complying in this life with these conditions are shortening their sentences, for every one of us will have a matter of years in that spirit state to complete

and finish their (sic) salvation. And some may attain, by
reason of their righteousness in this life, the right to do
postgraduate work, to be admitted into the Celestial
Kingdom, but others will lose absolutely the right to
that glory, all they can do will not avail after death to
bring them into the Celestial Kingdom.

The point I have in mind is that we are sentencing
ourselves to long periods of bondage, separating our spirits
from our bodies, or we are shortening that period,
according to the way in which we overcome and master
ourselves.[101]

After reading Elder Ballard's description, it is easy to
understand the importance of getting rid of every one of our negative
attitudes and characteristics. I am never happy after being impatient,
angry or arguing. I never experience joy after thinking or expressing
anything negative about anyone. Overcoming the propensity to do any
of these things is something to work on today. Maybe it will take
some time and much effort to weed these things out of my life. But it
will take me much less time and effort now than it will later. Because I
want to accomplish these positive changes in my life, I will dedicate
myself to succeeding—in conquering these undesirable traits—now.

It is very possible—maybe even very probable—that I will fail
repeatedly at making these changes. Therefore, I will add to my
personal resolve and efforts the one thing that will help insure my
success. I will sincerely pray to my Father in Heaven for His
assistance. I know He gave me my agency to choose for myself in all
things. I also know He will never change me without that being my
own decision. So not only will I make the decision to change, but in
my frequent and continuing prayers, I will both earnestly ask for His
help, AND, I will plead with Him and voluntarily authorize Him to
change my heart to bring about all of these changes (and any others I
need) in my own character, desires, feelings and personality traits. I
will literally turn my will over to Him, for I sincerely desire that I
become what He wills me to become. I can do this, for I know

without any doubt that His will is, and always will be, to bless me with everything good and wonderful that He can, everything that I can become worthy to receive from Him.

Combining these two elements will insure my success, if I remain resolved to do my part, to pick myself up whenever and however many times I fall or fail. I will remain resolved to keep trying and to keep asking for His help. I know the above statements and possibility of success through God's help to be true.

There are two wise sayings in which I firmly believe. First:

"One man with God is a majority."

Think about that. It does not matter if anyone should doubt me. With God—if my desires and actions are worthy of His approval and participation—I will always be in the majority, and this majority will always be right. The second saying is actually a quotation from an ancient prophet missionary, Ammon, who said:

Yea, I know that I am nothing; as to my strength I am weak; therefore I will not boast of myself, but I will boast of my God, for in His strength I can do all things; . . . [102]

Perhaps I—or you—will be incapable of overcoming our habits, desires, addictions or other weaknesses alone. But the Lord wants us to succeed just as much as we want to. Perhaps He wants it even more than we do. Despite that fact, He will not change us without two things—our authorization and our sincere and diligent participation. With both of those elements, He will do what we cannot do to help us succeed. If we ever quit trying, He will, of necessity, stop lifting us toward our goal. He cannot, as God, do for us what we can do for ourselves. But if we do all that we are able to do, He will do for us—lift and strengthen us—to accomplish what we are incapable of doing ourselves.

CHAPTER 16

THE SPIRIT WORLD

ACTIVITIES AND NATURE OF THE WICKED IN SPIRIT PRISON

"For the wages of sin is death; but the gift of God is eternal life through Jesus Christ our Lord."[103]

We all know the types of activities in which mortal men and women are engaged on Earth. But will the activities of the disembodied spirits differ greatly? The answer is both yes and no.

The extremely wicked, those who have spent their earthly days regularly engaged in debauchery and evil, will remain committed to pursuing the identical types of activities to the extent that they are able in the spirit world. Although limited in their actual ability to do so by virtue of their lack of a body, (as will be discussed hereinafter,) their desires, their methods of interaction with others and their character will remain constant. I will re-quote the third of three verses I have already quoted.

> Ye cannot say, when ye are brought to that awful
> crisis, that I will repent, that I will return to my God. Nay, ye
> cannot say this; for that same spirit which doth possess
> your bodies at the time that ye go out of this life, that same
> spirit will have power to possess your body in that eternal
> world.[104]

This same principle and admonition is stated in different words, with even greater emphasis in 2nd Peter in the New Testament:

> But these, as natural brute beasts, made to be taken
> and destroyed, speak evil of the things that they understand
> not; and shall utterly perish in their own corruption;
> And shall receive the reward of unrighteousness, as
> they that count it pleasure to riot in the day time. Spots they
> are and blemishes, sporting themselves with their own
> deceivings while they feast with you;
> Having eyes full of adultery, and that cannot cease
> from sin; beguiling unstable souls: an heart they have
> exercised with covetous practices; cursed children:
> Which have forsaken the right way, and are gone
> astray, following the way of Balaam the son of Bosor, who
> loved the wages of unrighteousness;
> These are wells without water, clouds that are carried
> with a tempest; to whom the mist of darkness is reserved
> forever.[105]

There are generally at least three distinct general levels of "wicked" in spirit prison. (1) The highest level is reserved for the less wicked spirits, those who have for the most part chosen to be good on Earth. They committed non-egregious sins but are uncommitted to the

Lord Jesus Christ and His authorized gospel. Some may even be called honorable men and women; (2) The middle level is for those who, as mortals, have committed non-malignant sins, more and/or greater in nature than those of the higher-level spirits. They are not as worthy as those in the higher level. Theirs are less evil sins than those of the lowest level, but they remain unrepentant of the wrongs they committed. In certain ways, they also did some good, but were satisfied with their unworthy status; (3) The lowest level is reserved for those who were evil on Earth.

I want to be clear about the distinction between these three levels in spirit prison. Scripturally, those who have not fully accepted the gospel of Jesus Christ, including baptism and other saving ordinances of the temple, can be referred to as unrighteous, or wicked. This is true even if these people were generally good or even honorable mortal beings. They are clearly better individuals than the people in each of the lower levels, who consciously chose wrong, or even evil deeds. They are better than those who did not seek to change for the better. They are certainly better than those who were evil and who could not by any stretch of the imagination be truthfully called good or honorable people.

These first, the least wicked, have generally been good people on Earth. They have not fully accepted the true gospel of Jesus Christ. They have not accepted or received the necessary saving ordinance of baptism by the proper authority. They may have been blinded by the craftiness of men. So, in a sense, they are wicked—not evil—maybe not even seriously wicked, not even unrepentant, but they have not completed all they are required to do to qualify for paradise. They are not wicked to the extent of the unrepentant wicked or of the extremely wicked, the evil doers. I will refer to these less wicked as "uncommitted" spirits, for they have not fully committed themselves to the Lord and the ordinances and covenants He requires. They will be in a separate part of spirit prison wherein they may pursue activities that their dispositions—brought with them from mortality—will lead them to do. We will discuss these spirits in greater detail in the next chapter.

The more wicked—unrepentant but not intentionally evil, will go to a lower level of spirit prison. Their level is still above the evil, those who intentionally followed Lucifer in doing evil to other people.

The very wicked—evil—remain in outer darkness, sometimes referred to as "hell," subject to the devil and his original, non-mortal, followers. They suffer in torment, having voluntarily subjected themselves on Earth to the devil's chains. They have rejected the gospel of Jesus Christ. They have chosen evil instead of good.

The prophet Joseph Smith said that one of the miseries experienced by those who did not apply themselves was to know they did not realize their spiritual potential during mortality:

> The great misery of departed spirits in the world of spirits, where they go after death, is to know that they come short of the glory that others enjoy and that they might have enjoyed themselves, and they are their own accusers.[106]

The unrepentant, evil spirits are restricted to districts away from the righteous and the less wicked, the boundaries of which are clearly defined and impassable by those evil spirits. As partially quoted elsewhere in this work, Elder Parley P. Pratt said of the unhappy, wicked spirits:

> Many spirits of the departed, who are unhappy, linger in lonely wretchedness about the earth, and in the air, and especially about their ancient homesteads, and the places rendered dear to them by the memory of the former scenes. . . .
>
> The more wicked of these are the kind spoken of in scripture, as "foul spirits," "unclean spirits," spirits who afflict persons in the flesh, and engender various diseases

in the human system. They will sometimes enter human bodies, and will distract them, throw them into fits, cast them into the water, into the fire, etc. They will trouble them with dreams, nightmares, hysterics, fever, etc. They will also deform them in body and in features, by convulsions, cramps, contortions, etc., and will sometimes compel them to utter blasphemies, horrible curses, and even words of other languages. . . .

Some of these spirits are adulterous, and suggest to the mind all manner of lasciviousness, all kinds of evil thoughts and temptations.[107]

Brigham Young spoke of their close proximity and the type of influence they can have on some mortals:

You may now see people with legions of evil spirits in and around them; there are men who walk our streets that have more than a hundred devils in them and round about them, prompting them to all manner of evil, and some too that profess to be Latter-day Saints, and if you were to take the devils out of them and from about them, you would leave them dead corpses; for I believe there would be nothing left of them.

I want you to understand these things; and if you should say or think that I know nothing about them, be pleased to find out and inform me. You can see the acts of these evil spirits in every place, the whole country is full of them, the whole earth is alive with them, and they are continually trying to get into the tabernacles of the human family, and are always on hand to prompt us to depart from the strict line of our duty.

You know that we sometimes need a prompter; . . . Well, these evil spirits are ready to prompt you. Do they prompt us? Yes, and I could put my hands on a dozen of them while I have been on this stand; they are here on the stand. . . . They are here, and they suggest this, that, and the other.[108]

Otherwise put, these wicked spirits, these former mortals, do not spend their time productively, doing those activities that will improve themselves or make themselves worthy of the Spirit of the Holy Ghost. Instead of learning those ennobling, saving things they so badly need, they spend their time pursuing the same evil and lascivious things they were so caught up in doing when they previously dwelled on Earth. They may even do so with much increased zeal and ferocity.

The prophet Moroni referred to these evil spirits and their mortal predecessors—still living in mortality—while he was writing to help us discern between good and evil. He wrote, in pertinent part:

> But whatsoever thing persuadeth men to do evil, and believe not in Christ, and deny him, and serve not God, then ye may know with a perfect knowledge it is of the devil; for after this manner doth the devil work, for persuadeth no man to do good, no, not one; neither do his angels; neither do they who subject themselves unto him.[109]

There are many who willingly "subject themselves unto Satan. We frequently see them on Earth. When they, or others like them, move into the spirit world—spirit prison—they may continue to follow their chosen dictator, Lucifer. Therefore, they seek to persuade us "to do evil, and believe not in Christ, and deny him, and serve not God," for through their actions and choices on Earth, they have become very much like their master, the devil.

In the spirit world, we will even retain the cravings, the addictions to which we voluntarily subject—even chain—ourselves while on Earth. Those horrible, controlling and dominating feelings will still control, dominate and chain our spirit in this next realm.

GLEN W. PARK

One medical doctor, George G. Ritchie, was serving in the military during World War II. He passed for a short time from mortal life to the spirit world. While out of his body, he was taken several places and shown some fascinating and terrifying things that spirit beings were experiencing as a result of their choices on Earth. His experiences and views in the spirit world complement and help us understand the teachings of prophets about this next realm in our existence. I quote with publisher's permission from his account:

I noticed this phenomenon repeatedly, people unaware of others right beside them.

I saw a group of assembly-line workers gathered around a coffee canteen. One of the women asked another for a cigarette, begged her in fact, as though she wanted it more than anything in the world.

But the other one, chatting with her friends, ignored her. She took a pack of cigarettes from her coveralls, and without ever offering it to the woman who reached for it so eagerly, took one out and lit it. Fast as a striking snake the woman who had been refused snatched at the lighted cigarette in the other one's mouth. Again she grabbed at it. And again . . .

With a little chill of recognition I saw that she was unable to grip it.

I thought of multiple experiences of seeing people who could pass through solid objects and who could not be heard by other, more solid, people, and myself yelling at a man who never turned to look at me.

And then I recalled the people here in this town trying in vain to attract attention, walking along a sidewalk without occupying space.

Clearly these individuals were in the same substance-less predicament I myself was in.

Like me, in fact, they were dead. . . .

Gradually, I began to notice something else.

88

All of the living people we were watching were surrounded by a faint luminous glow, almost like an electrical field over the surface of their bodies. This luminosity moved as they moved, like a second skin made out of pale, scarcely visible light.

At first I thought it must be reflected brightness from the Person at my side. But the buildings we entered gave off no reflection, neither did inanimate objects. And then I realized that the non-physical beings didn't either. My own un-solid body, I now saw, was without this glowing sheath.

At this point the Light drew me inside a dingy bar and grill near what looked like a large naval base. A crowd of people, many of them sailors, lined the bar three deep, while others jammed wooden booths along the wall. Though a few were drinking beer, most of them "seemed to be belting whiskies as fast as the two perspiring" bartenders could pour them.

Then I noticed a striking thing. A number of the men standing at the bar seemed unable to lift their drinks to their lips. Over and over I watched them clutch at their shot glasses, hands passing through the solid tumblers, through the heavy wooden counter top, through the very arms and bodies of the drinkers around them.

And these men, every one of them, lacked the aureole of light that surrounded the others.

Then, the cocoon of light must be a property of physical bodies only. The dead, we who had lost our solidness, had lost this "second skin" as well. And it was obvious that these living people, the light-surrounded ones, the ones actually drinking, talking, jostling each other, could neither see the desperately thirsty disembodied beings among them, nor feel their frantic pushing to get at those glasses. (Though it was also clear to me, watching, that the non-solid people could both see and hear each other. Furious quarrels were constantly breaking out among them over glasses that none could actually get to his lips.)

I thought I had seen heavy drinking at fraternity parties in Richmond, but the way civilians and servicemen at this bar were going at it beat everything. I watched one young sailor rise unsteadily from a stool, take two or three steps, and sag heavily to the floor.

Two of his buddies stooped down and started dragging him away from the crush.

But that was not what I was looking at. I was staring in amazement as the bright cocoon around the unconscious sailor simply opened up. It parted at the very crown of his head and began peeling away from his head, his shoulders. Instantly, quicker than I'd ever seen anyone move, one of the insubstantial beings who had been standing near him at the bar was on top of him. He had been hovering like a thirsty shadow at the sailor's side, greedily following every swallow the young man made. Now he seemed to spring at him like a beast of prey.

In the next instant, to my utter mystification, the springing figure had vanished. It all happened even before the two men had dragged their unconscious load from under the feet of those at the bar. One minute I'd distinctly seen two individuals; by the time they propped the sailor against the wall, there was only one.

Twice more, as I stared, stupefied, the identical scene was repeated. A man passed out, a crack swiftly opened in the aureole round him, one of the non-solid people vanished as he hurled himself at that opening, almost as if he had scrambled inside the other man.

Was that covering of light some kind of shield, then? Was it a protection against . . . against disembodied beings like myself? Presumably these substance-less creatures had once had solid bodies, as I myself had had. Suppose that when they had been in these bodies they had developed a dependence on alcohol that went beyond the physical. That became mental. Spiritual, even. Then when they lost that body, except when they could briefly take possession of another one, they would be cut off for all eternity from the thing they could never stop craving.

An eternity like that—the thought sent a chill shuddering through me—surely that would be a form of hell. I had always thought of hell, when I thought of it at all, as a fiery place somewhere beneath the earth where evil men like Hitler would burn forever. But what if one level of hell existed right here on the surface— unseen and unsuspected by the living people occupying the same space. What if it meant remaining on earth but never again able to make contact with it. I thought of that mother whose son couldn't hear her.

[Author's note: The mother had committed suicide, and was unceasingly pleading with the son she left behind to forgive her.]

The woman who wanted that cigarette. I thought of myself, caring only about getting to Richmond, unable to make anyone see me or help me. To want most, to burn with most desire, where you were most powerless—that would be hell indeed.

Not "would be," I realized with a start. Was. This was hell: . . .

But if this was hell, if there was no hope, then why was He here beside me? Why did my heart leap for joy each time I turned to Him? For He was overwhelmingly the chief impression of the journey.

All the sights and shocks assailing me were nothing compared to the main thing that was going on. Which was, quite simply, falling in love with the Person beside me.

And that was another of the things baffling me. If I could see Him, why couldn't everyone else? He was too bright for living eyes to look at—that I had realized right away. But surely the living people we passed must somehow sense the love streaming out to them like heat from a mighty fire!

And these others, the ones like me who no longer had physical eyes that could be destroyed, how could they help but see the burning Love and Compassion in their midst? How could they miss Someone closer, more brilliant than the noonday sun?

Unless . . .

For the first time it occurred to me to wonder whether something infinitely more important than I ever believed could have happened. . . . Was it possible that I, in some real way, had actually been . . . given new eyes, whether I understood any of it or not?

Or, could these others see Him now too, if their attention was not all caught up in the physical world they had lost? "Where your heart is. . . ." As long as my heart had been set on getting to Richmond by a certain date, I hadn't been able to see Jesus either. Maybe whenever our center of attention was on anything else, we could block out even Him.[110]

These poor, craving spirit beings had once been mortals on Earth. They had at one time moved about in solid, physical, mortal bodies. And during this, their time on Earth, they had developed such an addiction and dependence on either tobacco or alcohol, or both, that their enslavement to such substance(s) became more than merely physical. It had become deeper still. It was intellectual, emotional—in some sense—even spiritual. Obviously, for it was their body-less spirits that still craved the substances to which they were addicted while they had been in their mortal bodies. When death separated their addicted spirits from their addicted bodies, they were barred forever from the thing that would satisfy their cravings. These addictions would continue to enslave them and their minds and thoughts.

Spending any amount of time like that, and especially, an extended period, maybe a thousand years, or maybe even an eternity in such a dreadful circumstance, would surely be something that anyone would consider to be "hell." It certainly would be. It may well be even worse than the type of place the sectarian world normally thinks of as "hell."

This same doctor who temporarily viewed the world of spirits went on to describe the unsuccessful yet earnest efforts of spirits of the extremely wicked to fight, tear and hurt others around them. Although they were unable to actually inflict any real pain upon anyone else, they were still immersed, as it were, in a seeming fight to the death, trying every sort of maneuver to injure, put down, and gnash upon anyone and everyone within their limited realm. At first this doctor thought he was watching some great battle progressing, for everywhere he looked there were people who were totally absorbed in what appeared to be fights to the death. They were thrashing, hitting and tearing at each other. But upon looking more carefully, he could tell that it was not a present–day battle, for there was a total absence of any type of weapon. Imagine the types of weapons that people with such hatred and venom would use to carry out their outrage and lust for blood, if only they could. These combatants were locked in open battle, able to use only their hands, feet, mouths and teeth. And even stranger, it soon became evident that none of the fighters nor their intended victims were being injured. None were getting injured by the seemingly mortal battle in which they were engaged. No blood was being shed (for spirits have none to spill.) There were no bodies lying on the ground. When one would strike another with force that would normally be sufficient to immobilize the recipient, the result was totally harmless. The seemingly mortal blows were thoroughly impotent, ineffective. That fact only added to the frustration, anger and misery of the evil spirits whose capabilities were so limited because of their mortal wickedness.

Although the fighters in this spirit battle were right on top of each other, swinging their fists with the greatest ferocity, and although these blows were on target, in fact, the swings merely went through the air. These fighters were unable to even touch each other. So they were incapable of causing any actual injury to any other spirit. In the spirit world, spirits are not permitted to "actually" harm any other spirit.

They certainly wanted to maim, even kill the other. The sincerity of their hatred and desire to eliminate was real. Only their capability to exact their desired harm was lacking. In reality, their intended victims were already dead, so their continued horribly vicious efforts to inflict pain and death were useless. Their rage went unsatisfied. They were powerless, inept at doing the only thing they had become used to doing in mortal life—the only thing that seemed to matter to them—inflict harm on someone else. Their rage, being unsatisfied, remained undiminished. There seemed to be nothing else that they cared to do. But yet, they were totally incapable of even doing that which was their sole desire, the sole purpose in their life in the spirit world. Their "hell" included the complete inability to accomplish the only result they earnestly desired to achieve.

As I have already quoted from the writings of the apostle Melvin J. Ballard, "We will find when we are dead every desire, every feeling will be greatly intensified."[111]

There were others still who were wholly engaged in impotent, untellable actions perpetrated one upon another. Yet, although the actions were graphic and rotten, their result was totally lacking effect upon the victim. The observer could clearly hear their tormented sounds. But he could not discern whether their shrieking, bawling and yells of frustration were the result of being incapable of accomplishing their evil designs or if they were only the literal and audible utterances of the very thoughts of the individuals. For it was indeed not only possible to understand the thoughts and desires of the minds of these wretched spirit beings. Their thoughts were readily and openly available to be "heard," as it were, or maybe more correctly, understood and known by those who were near to anyone thinking any thoughts at all. And, amazingly, these thoughts carried from the thinker to the bystander or neighbor faster than words spoken by a mortal tongue could ever be transferred.

The type of thoughts being carried back and forth, continually spewing from the foul mouths and minds—beings—of these evil spirits were phrases and sentences to which we certainly would not want to be exposed for even moments, let alone a thousand years!

Those evil beings were fully caught up in their perverse thoughts and acts. They were totally immersed in their evil desires and lusts. They were riveted, even tied, to these thoughts and attempts to act out their perversions. But though they were entranced in their predisposed evil enterprises, they were completely inept at actually accomplishing them, for they could not actually perform as spirits that which they had voluntarily caused themselves to become addicted to, and enchained by, while on Earth.

These were chains of a different sort. The chains were not visible, not physical. Only their effects were visible. The habits, the hatred, the lusting, the evil and destructive preoccupations were in firm control of their minds and desires—every bit as much as they had been in these individuals while they were upon the Earth. The same spirit (type of character) they had developed on Earth remained with them in the next realm to which their spirits went after departing from their mortal frames. They remained filthy, evil still. They did not change from evil to righteous or from hurtful to beneficent.

Fortunately, the less wicked there—including the uncommitted—are not in the same part of spirit prison as such evil spirits as I have just described. Therefore, the less wicked also do not have to be exposed to those evil ones or their depravity.

So these are some of the potential activities of the wicked in spirit prison. Now all of these individuals were probably not the most wicked who had ever lived upon Earth in mortality. But while they were on Earth, their hearts were extremely riveted upon activities that were not ennobling. They were not at all focused upon the Savior, upon keeping themselves unspotted from the world or upon doing good continually. Whatever their focus was while on Earth remained their focus afterward. The invisible chains with which they got themselves bound on Earth, bound them still in the next world.

Certainly there could be other examples of the hearts of men pursuing their "treasures" while on the Earth and thereafter being set upon the same pursuits—but totally incapable of actually accomplishing any part of their earnest desires.

What about the man or woman whose greatest, maybe even only, desire on Earth was to read filthy books or to look upon pornographic materials? In the spirit world, no such books or materials exist in a form usable by the disembodied. If there are any earthly books or materials around, they cannot be opened or their pages turned by an unrighteous, non-physical, spirit being. Remember, nothing pure or spiritually interesting will satisfy the addiction to pornography or other unrighteous things of such spirit individuals.

What about the man or woman whose only desire is to spend time making money, climbing the ladder of worldly wealth or fame— he or she who seldom, if ever, took any thought to help out another or to lift another to a higher level? In the next realm, he or she would find it unpleasant, maybe unbearable, to be unable to have more than others or to satisfy their pride or pathetic desire for the glory of men. For where they will find themselves, such pursuits would yield nothing of the kind. They would be as unsuccessful as the attempts of the poor woman to snatch a cigarette with her spirit hand.

So, to those who have been prideful, self-centered and only focused on selfish or evil ends—those who willingly addicted themselves to any number of vices—the activities of the world of spirits will be miserable, unsatisfying and unfulfilling.

CHAPTER 17

THE SPIRIT WORLD

ACTIVITIES OF THE LESS WICKED: THE UNCOMMITTED IN SPIRIT PRISON

But God be thanked, that ye were the servants of sin, but ye have obeyed from the heart that form of doctrine which was delivered you.

Being then made free from sin ye became the servants of righteousness.

But now being made free from sin, and become servants to God, ye have your fruit unto holiness, and the end everlasting life.[112]

97

I will again use in this chapter's discussion the same set of verses I have quoted twice before. In addition to directly applying to what we will discuss herein, these verses are also excellent ones of which we all should keep being reminded.

> For behold, this life is the time for men to prepare to meet God; yea, behold the day of this life is the day for men to perform their labors.
> And now, as I said unto you before, as ye have had so many witnesses, therefore, I beseech of you that ye do not procrastinate the day of your repentance until the end; for after this day of life, which is given us to prepare for eternity, behold, if we do not improve our time while in this life, then cometh the night of darkness wherein there can be no labor performed.
> Ye cannot say, when ye are brought to that awful crisis, that I will repent, that I will return to my God. Nay, ye cannot say this; for that same spirit which doth possess your bodies at the time that ye go out of this life, that same spirit will have power to possess your body in that eternal world.[113]

These verses carry a far more vivid and forceful message to our heart and mind after having read the account of Dr. Ritchie and the poor spirits who remain addicted to, and afflicted by, the consequences of the choices they had made in mortality.

Now let us consider those who were wicked in a lesser way. These may have been pretty good or even very good people while on Earth. Their wickedness may have included non-heinous sins. One of their principal failings while on the Earth was that they were uncommitted—or even not yet committed—in one way or another, to the Lord Jesus Christ, His true teachings and commandments. They had failed to make and keep sacred covenants and to accept certain saving ordinances prescribed by the Lord Jesus Christ—maybe because they never had the chance on Earth. Their wickedness, if you will, was not pernicious. Like all of us, they certainly have committed sin. Their sins were both of commission and omission, although they were generally decent, and maybe even fine, people. Their failure to make and keep those essential covenants and accept those necessary saving ordinances may have even been because where and when they lived, those very ordinances were not available.

In the spirit world, these individuals will find themselves involved in certain seemingly temporal activities—gardening, reading, etc. But more importantly, when they discover for themselves that they need to have some additional spiritual instruction and do more to follow Christ, they will have the opportunity to be taught the truths of the gospel of Jesus Christ and avail themselves of its saving principles, covenants and ordinances. For there, they will find spirit representatives of the Lord, those who have been ordained and authorized to teach His gospel to all who are willing to hear that essential message. Clearly, it will be possible to improve their positions, to accept the truths of His gospel plan.

Of the continuing possibility of forgiveness, the Savior taught:

> . . . forgive, and ye shall be forgiven:[114]

> Wherefore I say unto you, All manner of sin and blasphemy shall be forgiven unto men: but the blasphemy against the Holy Ghost shall not be forgiven unto men.[115]

By His own statements, there are sins, even all manner of them that He will be willing to forgive in the world to come, the world of spirits. Because men are to be able to live in the spirit, but "be judged according to men in the flesh, . . ."[116] those spirit beings who could not be equally and fairly judged while they were on the Earth, will have the opportunity to hear and accept His gospel and its saving and ennobling truths in the spirit world, where they may indeed be forgiven "[a]ll manner of sin" in that world to come.

Peter tells us that following His crucifixion, Jesus

> . . . went and preached unto the spirits in prison,
> which sometimes were disobedient, when once the
> long–suffering of God waited in the days of Noah."[117]

What would you suppose He, or His servants taught them? Do you think they were informed that they were going to forever stay there, in prison? Were they to be told by Christ's representatives that they had no chance of ever moving to a better, higher place? Goodness no! It was the exact opposite.

Luke provides the scriptural answer to these questions:

> He hath sent me to heal the broken–hearted, to
> preach deliverance to the captives, and recovering of sight
> to the blind, to set at liberty them that are bruised.[118]

Isaiah also correctly taught this principle. He prophesied that the Savior would go "[t]o bring out the prisoners from the prison, and them that sit in darkness from the prison house."[119]

Christ, following His crucifixion, went, not only to preach to the spirits who were waiting captive. He also went to deliver them from that place, that prison house—all who would hear, accept and live the truths that He, through His authorized servants there, would teach to them. The prophet Alma taught his son the same principle, of Christ's mercy and of the absolute necessity of the atonement:

> And now, the plan of mercy could not be brought
> about except an atonement should be made; therefore
> God himself atoneth for the sins of the world, to bring about
> the plan of mercy, to appease the demands of justice, that
> God might be a perfect, just God, and a merciful God also. . . .
> . . . and mercy claimeth the penitent, and mercy
> cometh because of the atonement;

And the atonement bringeth to pass the resurrection of the dead; and the resurrection of the dead bringeth back men into the presence of God; and thus they are restored into his presence, to be judged according to their works, according to the law and justice.

And thus God bringeth about his great and eternal purposes, which were prepared from the foundation of the world. And thus cometh about the salvation and the redemption of men, and also their destruction and misery.

Therefore, O my son, whosoever will come may come and partake of the waters of life freely; and whosoever will not come the same is not compelled to come; but in the last day it shall be restored unto him according to his deeds.

If he has desired to do evil, and has not repented in his days, behold, evil shall be done unto him, according to the restoration of God.[120]

We see that the wicked shall have opportunities to be taught and embrace the gospel of Jesus Christ. They will have the chance to spend time in spirit prison seeking those things that bring with them the Spirit of the Holy Ghost, which Spirit Being shall surely have His influence available to all those who humble themselves and seek His help in discovering the truth. All of the instructions and the possibility of accepting vicarious ordinances will be available in the spirit world to the uncommitted—or not yet committed—all the teachings and saving ordinances of the gospel of Jesus Christ.

CHAPTER 18

THE SPIRIT WORLD

ACTIVITIES AND NATURE OF THE RIGHTEOUS SPIRITS IN PARADISE

Know ye not, that to whom ye yield yourselves servants to obey, his servants ye are to whom ye obey; whether of sin unto death, or of obedience unto righteousness?

But God be thanked, that ye were the servants of sin, but ye have obeyed from the heart that form of doctrine which was delivered you.

Being then made free from sin ye became the servants of righteousness.

But now being made free from sin, and become servants to God, ye have your fruit unto holiness, and the end everlasting life.[121]

I have again quoted from Romans, with one additional, relevant verse included. And again, I will re–state only the third verse of an introductory paragraph from prior chapters. We all know of the types of activities in which mortal men and women are engaged on Earth. But will the activities of the disembodied spirits differ greatly? The answer is both yes and no.

> Ye cannot say, when ye are brought to that awful crisis, that I will repent, that I will return to my God. Nay, ye cannot say this; for that same spirit which doth possess your bodies at the time that ye go out of this life, that same spirit will have power to possess your body in that eternal world.[122]

Although the wicked spirits in spirit prison are kept from being able to actually touch each other—primarily to keep one wicked being from hurting another, the righteous appear to not have any such restriction. The accounts of some spirit world visitors reveal that loved ones are able to embrace each other. The righteous have been seen walking or running hand in hand. Some have been transported by their spirit guides, who took the newcomer spirit by the hand and either floated or traveled at faster-than-the-speed-of-light speeds. The visiting spirit was able to feel the hand of his or her guide or loved one as they moved from one place to another. This seems reasonable, for the righteous can be trusted to treat others with respect and kindness, for among other reasons, they have matured sufficiently, both spiritually and emotionally, to be and to act at such a higher level in the first place.

Accounts indicate that righteous spirits have the sense of smell. Some temporary visitors have spoken or written of being able to smell the familiar scent of a loved one, which served to bring back memories and understanding of that loved one. Others have spoken or written of being able to smell the extraordinarily beautiful fragrance of flowers in the spirit realm.

Spirit bodies are filled with light. The brilliance of that light varies in spirit beings according to their degree of righteousness and their valiance in keeping the commandments of God while in the pre-existence, in mortality and in the spirit world. The Lord Jesus Christ and God our Father are the very brightest there. Those most like them are the next brightest, considerably more brilliant than others, whose brightness varies downward from them. There is some light in virtually all spirits in that paradisiacal spirit place. One can discern much about the level of obedience and God–like character by the very radiance of the spirit of each individual there.

Joseph Smith briefly described the state of righteous spirits:

> The spirits of the just are exalted to a greater and more glorious work; hence they are blessed in their departure to the world of spirits. Enveloped in flaming fire, they are not far from us, and know and understand our thoughts, feelings, and motions, and are often pained therewith.[123]

Those righteous individuals who were greatly involved in the work of the Lord upon the Earth, seeking the Spirit and Its direction in their lives, will find their activities in the spirit world to be very much like they were on Earth. There will be differences, of course—those related to the types of things that embodied people can and must do to make a living while on the Earth, versus those that spirit beings can and need to do. Otherwise, the nature of their earthly religious activities will be very similar to that of righteous spirits.

These righteous spirits will be involved in all kinds of righteous endeavors. Some, who are called to important positions of leadership in the work of the Lord, shall spend their time directing the work of teaching the gospel and administering in the ordinances thereof.

Other righteous spirits will spend much of their time in teaching those who have expressed an interest in, and willingness to hear, that gospel. Theirs will be a wonderful experience, for they will have wonderful, spirit–filled conversations and discussions focused on the eternal, life–saving principles and ordinances of the gospel. When the Spirit of the Holy Ghost is present and being felt, things are indeed wonderful. His presence and influence can and does lift one so that a hard experience can actually become a light– and peace–filled one. He can and does make an ordinary situation into a stimulating, remarkable one. This is the nature of the feelings and experiences that these righteous spirits will be having as they do these three things—(1) teach others the truths of the gospel; (2) receive instruction themselves in those things they need to know and do to complete their preparations for the glorious times and place that await them following their sojourn in the spirit world; and (3) perform other service as assigned there. They will continue in the service of their Master. They will pursue the remainder of the path remaining in their travel from the pre–existence to the glorious celestial realm prepared for those who love and follow the Lord, His teachings and His prescribed commandments.

The prophet Alma says it very concisely and well:

> And then shall it come to pass, that the spirits of those who are righteous are received into a state of happiness, which is called paradise, a state of rest, a state of peace, where they shall rest from all their troubles and from all care, and sorrow.[124]

Now this time and state of rest, this state of peace, will not be one spent languishing around, only playing harps and sitting on clouds, doing nothing in particular. Rather, it will be a time and state of "resting in the Lord," doing those things that will bring spiritual rest and peace, a mind–purifying and enlightening experience. For the righteous dead will spend their time in uplifting, enjoyable, stimulating and wholesome thoughts, activities and pursuits. In so doing, they will find themselves indeed uplifted, joyful, stimulated and wholesome— gloriously happy and fulfilled. They will also be about the work of the Lord in working to help accomplish all that must be done before the end of the millennial period, the resurrection and the final judgment.

Wilford Woodruff continued to receive instruction from Joseph Smith, even after the prophet's death. President Woodruff taught there is much to be done as he related his vision in which he spoke with the martyred prophet Joseph Smith:

> I saw him at the door of the temple in heaven. He came to me and spoke to me.
>
> He said he could not stop to talk with me because he was in a hurry. The next man I met was Father Smith [Joseph Smith Sr.]; he could not talk with me because he was in a hurry. I met half a dozen brethren who had held high positions on earth, and none of them could stop to talk with me because they were in a hurry. I was much astonished. By and by I saw the prophet again and I got the privilege of asking him a question.
>
> "Now," said I, "I want to know why you are in a hurry. I have been in a hurry all my life; but I expected my hurry would be over when I got into the kingdom of heaven, if I ever did."
>
> Joseph said: "I will tell you, Brother Woodruff. Every dispensation that has had the priesthood on the earth and has gone into the celestial kingdom has had a certain amount of work to do to prepare to go to the earth with the Savior when he goes to reign on the earth. Each dispensation has had ample time to do this work. We have not. We are the last dispensation, and so much work has to be done, and we need to be in a hurry in order to accomplish it."[125]

On July 4, 1892, President Joseph F. Smith, then second counselor in the First Presidency, explained some of the work that still must be done. He said:

> The millions and millions that have lived upon this earth and have passed away without the knowledge of the

Gospel here, will have to be taught them there, by virtue of the authority of this holy priesthood that you and I hold. The Church of God will be organized among them by the authority of this priesthood.[126]

President Joseph F. Smith taught how things will be for the righteous leaders chosen by the Lord on Earth. These righteous leaders will likewise be involved in the same work in the next world:

I have always believed, and still do believe with all my soul, that such men as Peter and James and the twelve disciples chosen by the Savior in his time, have been engaged all the centuries that have passed since their martyrdom for the testimony of Jesus Christ, in proclaiming liberty to the captives in the spirit world and in opening their prison doors. I do not believe that they could be employed in any greater work. Their special calling and anointing of the Lord himself was to save the world, to proclaim liberty to the captives, and the opening of the prison doors to those who were bound in chains of darkness, superstition, and ignorance. I believe that the disciples who have passed away in this dispensation—Joseph, the prophet, and his brother Hyrum, and Brigham, and Heber, and Willard, and Daniel and John, and Wilford and all the rest of the prophets who have lived in this dispensation, and who have been intimately associated with the work of redemption and the other ordinances of the gospel of the Son of God in this world, are preaching that same gospel that they lived and preached here, to those who are in darkness in the spirit world and who had not the knowledge before they went. The gospel must be preached to them. We are not perfect without them—they cannot be perfect without us.[127]

We have spoken much of the righteous men who have lived upon the Earth. Does the same apply to the righteous women who have lived on Earth? Absolutely! Just as the righteous men will be diligently involved in furthering the work of the Lord, "to bring to pass the immortality and eternal life of man,"[128] so will righteous women.

In his vision of the Savior's visit to the spirits of the dead, President Joseph F. Smith saw:

> Among the great and mighty ones who were assembled in this vast congregation of the righteous were Father Adam, the Ancient of Days and father of all.
> And our glorious Mother Eve, with many of her faithful daughters who had lived through the ages and worshiped the true and living God.[129]

Will there be only a few of such faithful daughters of Eve. Certainly not! In my opinion, there will likely be more righteous and faithful sisters who qualify to be there than there will be righteous men.

At a funeral, President Smith expanded our understanding of the teaching of the gospel in the spirit world to the sisters there:

> . . . at least one-half of those [in the spirit world] are women. Who is going to preach the Gospel to the women? Who is going to carry the testimony of Jesus Christ to the hearts of the women who have passed away without a knowledge of the Gospel? Well, to my mind, it is a simple thing. These good sisters who have been set apart, ordained to the work, called to it, authorized by the authority of the holy priesthood to minister, for their sex, in the House of God for the living and for the dead, will be fully authorized and empowered to preach the Gospel and minister to the women while the elders and prophets are preaching it to the men.[130]

The spirit world is made up of the billions of spirits who have come to the Earth for their mortal body, experiences and tests. Most then passed on from mortality without having received a correct understanding of the gospel of Jesus Christ. At least half of them would be female. As I said above, it would not surprise me if many more than half would be women. Many faithful women have been authorized to teach the gospel and administer in the ordinances of the temple on Earth. They will be called and set apart in the world of spirits to preach the gospel, and to assist their fellow sisters, daughters of our Father in Heaven, in coming to the knowledge of the gospel there. I believe things on Earth were created in a manner like unto the pre−existent world from which we have come. Similarly, the world that follows Earth's mortal existence will be very much like both our pre−existent and mortal worlds. The major difference in the spirit world will be the absence of Satan's influence or control over any aspect of the continuing lives of the good and righteous spirits there.

On Earth, faithful women teach other sisters in both Young Women and Relief Society. God's kingdom on Earth is patterned after God's kingdom—both that part from which we came to Earth, and that part to which we hope to go after mortality.

President Joseph F. Smith confirmed this concept. He said: "The things we experience here are typical of the things of God and the life beyond us."[131]

God, our Father, knows all things. Therefore, it would be accurate, though understatement, to say that He is extremely, even supremely, intelligent. He, possessing such extraordinary intelligence and knowledge, would certainly not dwell in a less−than−great or intelligent type of place. He would not choose to have His most righteous servants do His work somewhere that was not as good a place as He could easily make available for them. And He would certainly establish a means for teaching His gospel in a way that He knows is the most effective in touching the hearts of His sincere and faithful children, for whom He has great love. He would not do it in some other, less−effective way. I am totally confident that He knows the best way to preserve for His beloved children their agency to choose for themselves the course they will take. I am likewise confident He has established and used that best way to teach His beloved children, still requiring them to exercise faith and allowing them their agency to choose whether to accept those teachings. He is all-knowing. He is all–wise. He is also all–loving. Being all of those things, He would only choose the best, most effective and loving way to allow His beloved spirit children every opportunity possible to exercise faith and their agency to hear and accept His eternal life–giving truths and ordinances.

He has done so already on Earth. I believe His methods of trying to reach His children to allow them to exercise both their agency and faith in accepting His true and living gospel will certainly be very much the same in the next realm as it has been here on Earth.

CHAPTER 19

THE SPIRIT WORLD

ADDITIONAL ACTIVITIES OF THE RIGHTEOUS

Although the spirit world will be a place of peace, spirits there will still have responsibilities. What are the main types of activities in which righteous spirit beings will be involved? I will first list, then describe many of the most important of those listed activities. The righteous spirits in paradise will be diligently involved in accomplishing a number of eternally worthwhile and important activities:

(1) Increasing their own knowledge and understanding of God and of His nature and works; (2) Related to #1 above, and perhaps included in it, is increasing their knowledge and understanding of all things—science, biology, chemistry and physics, horticulture, agriculture, music, literature, languages—just to name a few; (3) Teaching others who are numbered among the righteous in paradise; (4) Teaching others who are less righteous, and still in spirit prison, as some from paradise are assigned to take the saving truths to those in

111

spirit prison who have not yet had the full opportunity to hear or accept them; (5) Assisting in the gathering of genealogical information—either on the spirit world side or the Earth side, or both; (6) Assisting in the accomplishment of important events that are still to come on Earth; (7) Assisting as ministering spirits to others in the spirit world who have already achieved a higher level; (8) Assisting as ministering spirits—angels—to people on Earth; (9) Performing service, including as groups performing as angelic choirs in the spirit world and on Earth; (10) Performing other assignments as received from those in authority there, assignments that will help to bring about the successful accomplishment of the vast expanse of the Lord's work necessary before the Master can declare, "The work is done."

Now let us consider each of these just briefly.

(1) Increasing their own knowledge and understanding of God and of His nature and works. One of the principal pursuits of the righteous there will be the acquisition of knowledge of godly things. Joseph Smith offered this clarifying teaching:

> Here, then, is eternal life—to know the only wise and true God; and you have got to learn how to be gods yourselves, and to be kings and priests to God, the same as all gods have done before you, namely, by going from one small degree to another, and from a small capacity to a great one; from grace to grace, from exaltation to exaltation, until you attain to the resurrection of the dead, and are able to dwell in everlasting burnings, and to sit in glory, as do those who sit enthroned in everlasting power.[132]

In his discourse at the funeral of King Follett, he further stated:

> Knowledge saves a man; and in the world of spirits no man can be exalted but by knowledge. So long as a man will not give heed to the commandments, he must abide

without salvation. If a man has knowledge, he can be saved; although, if he has been guilty of great sins, he will be punished for them. But when he consents to obey the gospel, whether here or in the world of spirits, he is saved.[133]

Brigham Young added:

. . . then we shall go on from step to step, from rejoicing to rejoicing, and from one intelligence and power to another, our happiness becoming more and more exquisite and sensible as we proceed in the words and powers of life.[134]

He further stated:

If we are striving with all the powers and faculties God has given us to improve upon our talents, to prepare ourselves to dwell in eternal life, and the grave receives our bodies while we are thus engaged, with what disposition will our spirits enter their next state? They will be still striving to do the things of God, only in a much greater degree—learning, increasing, growing in grace and in the knowledge of the truth.[135]

(2) Increasing their knowledge and understanding of all things—science, biology, chemistry, physics, horticulture, agriculture, music, literature, languages, just to name a few. I readily acknowledge that God, our Father, knows everything. That is the definition of omniscient. That "everything" is not just as to spiritual or religious matters. It literally is everything. He knows everything about physics, medicine, horticulture—everything. In our efforts to become more and more as He is, we also need to know more and more about—well—everything. So we will also spend "time"—which is a mortal-world term—learning about all things.

As stated above, the revelation in The Doctrine and Covenants, Section 93 teaches the importance of knowledge and explains the way to best obtain it—in fact—to learn about all things:

> And no man receiveth a fulness unless he keepeth his commandments.
> He that keepeth his commandments receiveth truth and light, until he is glorified in truth and knoweth all things.[136]

So the way to come to know all things (which is quite an accomplishment!) is to keep God's commandments. How does obedience bring one to know everything? The prophet Moroni helps us to piece together this puzzle. He teaches: "And by the power of the Holy Ghost ye may know the truth of all things."[137]

If we want to learn truth—indeed "the truth of all things"—by the power of the Holy Ghost, it is easy to determine that the best, most certain, way to learn real truth is to have the Holy Spirit with us.

Indeed, the early apostles showed that the Holy Ghost was very important. When the apostles Peter and John went to Samaria, that had received the word of God, we are taught:

> Who, [referring to Peter and John] when they were come down, prayed for them, that they might receive the Holy Ghost: . . . Then laid they their hands on them, and they received the Holy Ghost.[138]

In February 1847, Brigham Young saw Joseph Smith in a dream or vision, in which the prophet Joseph instructed:

> Tell the people to be humble and faithful, and be sure to keep the spirit of the Lord and it will lead them right. Be careful and not turn away the small still voice; it will teach you what to do and where to go; it will yield the fruits of the kingdom. Tell the brethren to keep their

hearts open to conviction, so that when the Holy Ghost comes to them, their hearts will be ready to receive it.

The prophet further directed Brigham Young as follows:

They can tell the Spirit of the Lord from all other spirits; it will whisper peace and joy to their souls; it will take malice, hatred, strife and all evil from their hearts; and their whole desire will be to do good, bring forth righteousness and build up the kingdom of God.[139]

The Holy Ghost does teach all truth, including the most important of all—that Jesus is the Christ, the divine Son of God.

But the Holy Ghost does not remain with anyone who is unworthy of His presence. The prophet Nephi explains, ". . . the Spirit of the Lord . . . had withdrawn from them because the Spirit of the Lord doth not dwell in unholy temples."[140] Thus we see the reason to keep God's commandments—that is the only way to be worthy of the ongoing presence, inspiration and assistance of the Holy Ghost. When we keep the Lord's commandments, we may have the blessing of the presence and direction of the Holy Ghost. With that assistance, as we apply ourselves to learn truth—any truth—we will best be able to obtain that knowledge and full understanding.

(3) Teaching others who are numbered among the righteous in paradise. Whether we wish to learn gospel-related truth, or truth pertaining to physics, music or other matters, we will be instructed by other inhabitants of paradise. We may well instruct others in areas in which we have come to excel. Books and other materials will also be available. If we want to become great, to know what God knows, we will need to acquire knowledge of all things. As stated before, our spirits will be able to grasp the very thoughts and experiences of the authors of the materials we "read." Therefore, we will thoroughly learn all of the elements of each topic we study, and with incredible speed.

Remember what we learned from the account of Lawrence Tooley and his visit to the spirit world. Everyone in the spirit world thirsts for knowledge. Spirits reap great joy in pursuing knowledge. (See p. 72 of this book.) His guide then told Larry:

> ... If we're going to inherit Father's Kingdom, we need to be intelligent enough to administer in the affairs of the Kingdom.[141]

(4) Teaching others who are less righteous and in spirit prison, as some from paradise are assigned to teach saving truths to those who have not yet had the full opportunity to hear or accept them. We may be assigned to go to a lower level in the spirit world, even spirit prison, to teach the essential saving principles and ordinances to those who have prepared themselves and are desirous to hear such important teachings. This assignment or calling will require one to travel—a speedy process—from the paradisiacal realm to that lower realm, and then to return to paradise on a repeated basis as the teaching continues.

Apostle Bruce R. McKonkie wrote of this great effort of teaching those spirits who are less righteous:

> The great work in the world of spirits is the preaching of the gospel to those who are imprisoned by sin and false traditions."[142]

We learn more of the work of faithful spirits from a number of sources. In The Doctrine and Covenants, we are told that from paradise in the spirit world, faithful elders and sisters who have departed this life will continue their work in preaching the gospel of repentance and redemption among those who are in darkness in spirit prison.[143]

Of the certainty that the gospel of Jesus Christ will be taught to every one of the children of our Father in Heaven, Joseph F. Smith explained:

> Not one dead or living person will pass beyond the
> Father's notice, or will be left without hope. They will be
> brought to where they may receive the fullness of the
> Gospel, that they may be saved and exalted in the
> presence of God; or, rejecting that, they become the
> sons of perdition and heirs of destruction. . . . There are
> millions on millions that have died without the knowledge
> of the Gospel who are as worthy of salvation as you or I
> are worthy. . . . As Jesus went to preach the Gospel to
> the antediluvians while his body lay in the tomb, so are
> Joseph the prophet, President Young, President Taylor,
> and the Apostles that have died in this age in possession
> of the testimony of the truth, today preaching to the
> millions that have passed behind the veil without the
> knowledge of the Gospel.[144]

(5) Assisting either on the spirit world side or the Earth side, or both, the gathering and assembling of genealogical information. There are billions of spirit children of God who have lived and who will yet live on Earth. Most of them have not had the opportunity to learn the saving truths of the gospel of Jesus Christ. In addition to the necessity of each having that opportunity, the actual physical accomplishment of the ordinances vicariously on Earth for them will proceed for the next one thousand years of the millennium. The searching out of their names has been proceeding for some time on Earth. But many billions have lived upon the Earth, and for many, there exists no earthly or physical record of their birth, life or death. But records have been kept in the spirit world of every soul who has passed through the pre–existence, on to mortality on Earth and then to the world of spirits. There are spirits in the world of spirits who will be collecting and transmitting that information to individuals on Earth who are working on this side of the veil to complete the Earth—or physical—part of the work required by the Lord.

There is an account of a faithful man in the late 1800's who was earnestly seeking to find the names and other relevant information about certain of his kindred dead who had lived in England. He earnestly sought the Lord's help with this righteous desire. After some period of effort, one morning as he was about to enter the Manti, Utah Temple, he was approached by a man who handed him a newspaper that was from the very area of England where these deceased ancestors had lived. He noticed that the publication date of the newspaper was the very day he received it. There was no way he could have received a newspaper dated that same day and morning from England, except through heavenly or angelic assistance—using righteous spirits' ability to travel faster than the speed of light. Intrigued, he thumbed through the pages and discovered the names and other needed information about the very ancestors for whom he had so diligently been searching.[145]

(6) Preparing for and assisting in the accomplishment of important events that are still to come on Earth. There are many important events occurring, and yet to occur on Earth, for which spirits are working to have things prepared. One example of this has just been given. In anticipation of the building of additional temples on Earth, and the consequent increased capacity to perform more and more vicarious temple ordinances for those who have passed on, spirit beings in the spirit world are busy preparing lists of names, and transmitting them to mortal individuals charged with completing this Earth-side part of their work. Others will be doing that which is necessary to be ready for additional spirits who are continually leaving mortality and entering the spirit world. Undoubtedly, many things must be accomplished in order to continually be prepared for this influx of additional spirits in that realm. Plus, one can only imagine— perhaps one cannot even imagine—what preparatory work must be done to organize matters and the spirits who will be involved in the great second coming of the Savior.

(7) Assisting as ministering spirits to others in the spirit world who have already achieved a higher level. Good and just individuals

will be blessed as they serve those beings who have already achieved a higher—or much higher—level of perfection. The prophet Brigham Young spoke of these following the death of James Adams, saying:

> The spirits of just men are made ministering servants to those who are sealed unto life eternal, and it is through them that the sealing power comes down. . . . The spirits of the just are exalted to a greater and more glorious work; thence they are blessed in their departure to the world of spirits.[146]

(8) Assisting as ministering spirits—angels—to people on Earth. Many faithful individuals in paradise will be assigned to serve as ministering angels to mortals on Earth.

If the ministering assignment is of universal application—for the entire church or world—it will likely be carried out by one of the Lord's prophets. For individual mortals on Earth, the ministering angels called to assist them are generally their kindred or friends who already feel love and concern for them. No other spirit cares about us as much or can bring a message filled with love and personal meaning as will someone who on Earth developed tender feelings for us here.

Speaking of such ministering angels—spirits—President Joseph F. Smith said:

> We are told by the prophet Joseph Smith, that "there are no angels who minister to this earth but those who do belong or have belonged to it." Hence, when messengers are sent to minister to the inhabitants of this earth, they are not strangers, but from the ranks of our kindred, friends, and fellow-beings and fellow-servants . . . Our fathers and mothers, brothers, sisters and friends who have passed away from this earth, having been faithful, and worthy to enjoy these rights and privileges, may

have a mission given them to visit their relatives and friends
upon the earth again, bringing from the divine Presence
messages of love, of warning, or reproof and instruction, to
those whom they had learned to love in the flesh.[147]

(9) Performing service, including in groups performing as
angelic choirs in the spirit world and on Earth. There have been
numerous occasions on Earth at which angelic or heavenly choirs have
been heard. This was the case at the dedication of the Kirtland, Ohio
Temple. The day following that dedication, many met together to
recount the experiences they had had and the things they had seen and
heard at the dedication. The prophet Joseph Smith recorded:

> The Heavens were opened to Elder Sylvester Smith,
> And he leaped up exclaiming "The horsemen of Israel and
> the Chariots thereof. . ." . . . The gift of tongues fell upon
> us in mighty power. Angels mingled their voices with ours,
> while their presence was in our midst, and unceasing
> praises swelled our bosoms for the space of half an hour.[148]

Surely, the spirit beings who performed these and other choral
presentations did so after adequate preparation in the spirit realm. No
reasonable consideration of heavenly choirs would assume that they
haphazardly gave their presentation without the precision and beauty
of a well-rehearsed and organized choir.

There are certainly other types of work assigned to spirit beings
for which those beings need to do or learn something, to be fully
prepared to accomplish that work in the manner that everyone would
expect a representative or group of representatives of the Lord to do.

(10) Performing other assignments as received from those in
authority there, assignments that will help to bring about the successful
accomplishment of the vast expanse of the Lord's work, necessary
before the Master can declare, "The work is done." There are surely

many additional assignments that are regularly given to spirit inhabitants of paradise. Biblical accounts of such would include the appearance of the angel Gabriel to the Virgin Mary. That same angel Gabriel appeared to Zechariah, the husband of Mary's cousin, Elisabeth, to announce that Elisabeth would become pregnant. She would give birth to the prophet sent to prepare the way for the coming of the Lord—even John the Baptist.[149]

An angel appeared to Alma the younger while he was traveling with the sons of Mosiah. His appearance was in answer to the prayers of Alma's father, Alma, in behalf of his rebellious son. His message ultimately lead the younger Alma to repent and seek to serve the Lord.[150]

Later, in the Book of Alma, the same angel appeared to a repented, righteous Alma and delivered this message:

> Blessed are thou, Alma; therefore, lift up thy head and rejoice, for thou hast great cause to rejoice, for thou hast been faithful in keeping the commandments of God from the time which thou receivedst thy first message from him. Behold, I am he that delivered it unto you.[151]

There are undoubtedly other assignments that will be given to the righteous spirits by the Lord and His authorized servants, for there is much to be done before the work of the Lord, "to bring to pass the immortality and eternal life of man"[152] is completed.

CHAPTER 20

THE SPIRIT WORLD

THE AMAZING BEAUTY OF THIS PLACE

But as it is written, Eye hath not seen, nor ear heard, neither have entered into the heart of man, the things which God hath prepared for them that love him."[153]

Now let us consider how this place called paradise will look. The spirit world is a place of extraordinary beauty. I believe the Apostle Paul was correct in his above–quoted statement. Our mortal eyes have not seen, our mortal ears have not heard and there has not even entered into our earthly hearts how great, how glorious, how wonderful and beautiful are the things and the places our loving God has prepared. He prepared them for those who love Him and who have shown that love by their diligence in following His commandments while on Earth. Remember Christ's statement: "If ye love me, keep my commandments."[154] Obedience is the first law in heaven. It is how we show Him that we truly love Him.

According to the accounts of multiple individuals who have temporarily passed from "this side" to "that side" of the veil, I will attempt to explain the types of beauties, abundance and glories we will find there.[155] These beautiful settings will be present for all those who go there, having shown themselves to be righteous and diligent followers of the Lord Jesus Christ. In attempting to do this, I found that my human vocabulary was terribly inadequate to properly describe the images there to be seen. Indeed, the English language—all earthly languages, in fact—are inadequate for the task. This place of transcendent beauty is beyond, even defies earthly descriptions. But I must try, nonetheless. Therefore, I will repeatedly use words such as "beauty," "beautiful," "glorious," "amazing," "pretty," "peaceful" and "wonderful" in my attempts to describe the amazing (there I go!) surroundings there. These words, and others like them, are insufficient to accurately portray just how glorious is this place prepared for the righteous. My attempt will, nonetheless, have to suffice, for I am incapable of doing better in my mortal descriptions of the beauties of the beyond-mortal, heavenly spirit world.

Those who have a place reserved there for them will have such because of their firm obedience and conscientious efforts to serve the Lord and their fellow men while on Earth. They will find themselves in the midst of such glorious and beautiful surroundings that they will undoubtedly be overwhelmed with the wonder and indescribable beauty. The following are descriptions taken from accounts given by individuals who have temporarily looked into the spirit world— generally what are referred to as (1) "visions" or (2) "near-death experiences."

Many individuals' accounts of their visions of, or experiences in, the spirit world mention trees, shrubs and other foliage. President George Albert Smith described what he saw in the spirit world in vision or in the spirit. He said:

A number of years ago I was seriously ill, in fact, I think everyone gave me up but my wife. . . . I became so weak as to be scarcely able to move. It was a slow and exhausting effort for me even to turn over in bed.

One day, under these conditions, I lost consciousness of my surroundings and thought I had passed to the other side.

I found myself standing with my back to a large and beautiful lake, facing a great forest of trees. There was no one in sight, and there was no boat upon the lake or any other visible means to indicate how I might have arrived there. I realized, or seemed to realize, that I had finished my work in mortality and had gone home.

I began to look around, to see if I could not find someone. There was no evidence of anyone living there, just those great, beautiful trees in front of me and the wonderful lake behind me.

I began to explore, and soon I found a trail through the woods which seemed to have been used very little, and which was almost obscured by grass. I followed this trail, and after I had walked for some time and traveled a considerable distance through the forest, I saw a man coming towards me.[156]

In some areas, there are snow white, marble-like pebbles that make up the pathways. As far as the eye can see, the amply–wide and pretty paths extend. In some places, the fields that line either side of these pathways are beautiful, waving grain. This wonderful scene extends far into the distance.

At other places, not really that far away, the impressive pathway will lead to a beautiful forest, but not just one with grand trees. Of course, there are wonderfully impressive and grand trees, but these are surrounded by a pretty and pleasant carpet of lawn–like grass that covers the ground around and between the trees. In addition to trees and grass, there are other shrubs, beautiful in their own right, located and arranged in such a way as to enhance the beauty and complement the arrangement of the trees and grasses.

Moreover, there is not just one variety, size, kind or color of trees, flowers, grass or shrubs. Although they all complement and harmonize with each other, there are many different sizes, kinds, arrangements and colors of each of these types of flora. In fact, the numbers of varieties and combinations is apparently almost endless.

We are accustomed to having only green grass, which we rightly consider to be beautiful. But in the spirit world, where the righteous go to dwell for a time prior to their resurrection, the trees, the shrubs and the grasses and flowers are of many different colorings. In some sections, we will find pale green, and even changing gradations of hue all the way to deep green. In other areas, we will find even numerous shades of gold, silver, red, blue, pink, brown and lavender. And in the various sectors, it is not just the flowers that are these beautiful, bright and differing colorings. The grasses, themselves, are in some places one shade of lavender, for example. And then in another place, the grass is a different shade, either lighter or darker than in the other areas. And where one grass is of one color and shade, the shrubs and trees there harmonize perfectly and beautifully with that color and shade of grass.

Being at certain vantage points, one can literally look in one direction and see all of the vivid colors and shades of a rainbow, set together to harmonize in the most beautiful way! The colors are totally beyond description in earthly words. One description would have us try to come close to what is found there by using a crystal through which to view a rainbow and its varied and beautiful tones and shades. The trees, shrubs and flowers even seem to have their own personalities. Energy emanates from them all. There is even a glow, a light that comes from inside these gorgeous forms of plant life.[157], [158], [159]

We all may feel that we have seen beautiful gardens, forests and fields on earth. But we have not seen anything yet!

Jedediah M. Grant, an apostle and counselor to President Brigham Young, having viewed the glorious beauty of paradise, reported:

> I have seen good gardens on this earth, but I never saw any to compare with those that were there. I saw flowers of numerous kinds, and some with from fifty to a hundred different colored flowers growing upon one stalk.[160]

What awaits us, if we are worthy to go to this part of the world of spirits, is beyond our wildest—and even beyond our most creative imagination!

We will be able to continue on, thinking we have really seen about all of the beauty possible, and then we will come to other districts in which we will find the most magnificent flower gardens imaginable. The flowers are of all types, sizes, colors and shades. But this is not all. They are placed in numerous artistic designs. Some are arranged in the shapes of diamonds, some in crescents and some in ovals. Still others are in square shapes, others in oblongs. There are still many other additional shapes and configurations. The flowers are arranged, as to color, shade, shape and combination so as to enhance the splendor, radiance and beauty of their surroundings.

As to the size of these flowers—some are as small as the head of a pin! Some of the flowers are as large as a cereal bowl. And obviously, all of these grasses, trees, shrubs and flowers are kept trimmed and pruned so as to contribute to the maximum beauty and magnificence possible.

Many shrubs and flowers are trimmed and pruned to be in the shapes of animals and birds. And their shapes and sizes are made to be true to life. Ponder the material of which their eyes—that is, the eyes of these flower-animals are made. Their eyes appear to be made of real diamonds and rubies! Imagine, if you can, all different types and colors of plants, including even cactus plants, trained to grow in the shapes of all kinds of animals, birds and reptiles, possessing eyes of beautiful and complementary precious stones.

Picture an elephant, as large as life, composed of plants and shrubs, supported by four shrub legs growing out of the ground. Its head, trunk, tail and tusks are all made up of sculpted plants and shrubs. Even its ears are real-life size, and flat—perfect in design and image. Its eyes are there, too, made of small blue diamonds! The tusks are ivory in color, of course, but are entirely made up of plant life.

There are gorgeous flowering trees. Their configuration and beauty are far beyond anything man has ever seen on earth. Some such trees have numerous branches that spread outward and upward from the trunks. These branches appear like a giant flowerpot. And then above these gorgeous, vase–like branches, we see magnificent flowers—but on each of these branches are flowers of the same type, but of differing colors. So, there before our eyes is a veritable rainbow of impressive flowers, all on the same tree, the branches of which even make up its own vase to hold this bright and beautiful array. To even further enhance the beauty thereof, coming from the base of each flower is a fine fern leaf with different shades that serve to harmonize and complement the coloration of the flower in that particular spot on each branch.

The colors cannot be adequately described with earthly language. As previously noted, one individual who witnessed the overwhelming beauty said that to get an obscure, imperfect idea of the expanse of colors to be seen there, one could look at a rainbow through a clear crystal. But even then, the colors one would see are not nearly as vivid or bright as the colors in the spirit world. Such vividness would exist for at least two reasons: (1) one's "spirit" eyes are not clouded by mortal restrictions; and (2) things in paradise are indeed more marvelous than mortal materials.

Moreover, every flower, tree and shrub, even every blade of grass glows from within itself. Each of these separate beautiful items has its very own personality, with power and energy forces coming from inside them.[161]

I believe it entirely accurate to say that the faithful and obedient have awaiting them in the spirit world more beautiful kinds of plant life, all prepared to harmonize and complement each other, far surpassing anything and everything that the most capable and creative florists, gardeners, and landscape architects have ever dreamed of. For the possibilities that are and will be in the world of spirits exceed by so far, anything which is even remotely possible to do on Earth.

I have just made an inadequate attempt to describe in some small detail what we will find in the part of the spirit world where the righteous will be found. We will see shrubs and all kinds of plants that are humanly impossible to adequately describe. But, using all of the admiringly-descriptive words that man's vocabulary can muster, I merely come up with inadequate words, such as: exquisite, wonderful, awesome, gorgeous, and beautiful. All of these words are correct. They simply are not good enough. They simply do not do justice to what our eyes—indeed our entire spirits—will behold.

Now, please try to conceive in your mind one additional extension to the visual beauty that will present itself to our spirit eyes there—if we are worthy enough to go there. Not only will there be extraordinary shades, colors, species, combinations and variations. But, as is herein explained, our spirit eyes will not be fettered by the same limiting acuity that mortal eyes possess. In other words, the difference in our ability to see there, as compared to our ability to see on Earth, will be much greater than the difference in one's ability on Earth to see without corrective lenses, having 20/200 vision, versus having 20/20 vision! So the overwhelmingly greater beauty and grandeur there will be even multiplied and enhanced by one's ability to see so very much more clearly, distinctly and fully as glorified spirits.

Even the sky is more vivid and attractive than any earthly sky. And that is really saying something, for I have seen many truly beautiful skies during my life. But in the spirit world, the sky is a radiant, deep and vivid blue, deeper blue in color than ever could be seen on earth. The water is crystal clear and shimmering blue.

I envision beautiful, uplifting music can be both heard and felt in the glorious paradisiacal parts of the spirit world. It seems to come from everywhere, and yet is so subtle and quiet as to not disturb or disrupt. It just adds a pleasant, soothing and spiritual feeling and influence to the glorious surroundings. Some have heard a throng of beautiful voices, as well as a myriad of instruments that harmonize most majestically. Even the songs of the birds and other sounds blend with the music to be a complementary part of the whole. It could even be said that part of what was resonating from the music was love and peace. And just as with all of the other wonderful "things" in this glorious place, the music is not merely heard through one's ears. It is sensed in the entire being of the spirits there.

Lawrence Tooley wrote of the beautiful music he became aware of in his visit to the spirit world:

> . . . I could faintly hear music, and yet I could feel the music vibrating through me too . . . a . . . melodic musical symphony. . . . I could feel and hear it coming from . . . every direction and from every object. I felt on the verge of tears with the sheer ecstasy . . .[162]

Elane Durham also described the beautiful music she heard in the spirit world—music that included both choral and instrumental sounds:

> There was a sound in the air that completely defies description. It was as if there were a multitude of voices, and a multitude of instruments, blended and playing soft music. The twittering of birds and other beautiful sounds were all melodically instrumented into the music which wafted through the air. The sounds just flowed into me in a soft, soft manner.[163]

Other accounts, not quoted herein, also spoke of hearing choirs. One even compared its sound to that of the Mormon Tabernacle Choir.[164]

Now let us briefly consider the types of buildings, sidewalks and streets that will greet the righteous entrant there. The streets are beautifully paved and wide. The homes and other buildings—for there are definitely other buildings there—are also impressive. There are parks, playgrounds, and other places of rest and enjoyment, exceedingly pleasing to the eyes and ears, and peaceful and comforting to the mind and spirit. The most ordinary, or in other words, the least impressive of the spirit world buildings are vastly superior and more impressive than Solomon's Temple, which was known for its extraordinary beauty, even filled with gold and silver.

President Heber C. Kimball, speaking of President Jedediah M. Grant's vision of the spirit world, recounted:

> He also spoke of the buildings he saw there, remarking that the Lord gave Solomon wisdom and poured gold and silver into his hands that he might display his skill and ability, and said that the temple erected by Solomon was much inferior to the most ordinary buildings he saw in the spirit world.[165]

Many buildings, and the benches and walls within, are made of white crystallized marble. The appearance and feeling inside them is very soft and pleasant to the senses of the inhabitants there. The same crystallized materials are used in many buildings. But each one is of a different color, and each has the same soft, soothing feeling.[166]

In this glorious neighborhood are magnificent chapels and public meeting places. And just as one would suspect, these places are surrounded by, and some even covered by, attractive vines and climbing flowers. They are most inviting and pleasant to see. And inside, their beauty and attractiveness are expanded by the peace, serenity and uplifting spirit that fill their interiors. And there are even gloriously   beautiful   temples   found   in   these   wonderful neighborhoods.[167]

After an accident that caused serious injuries to him, Lance Richardson remained in a drug-induced coma for an extended period of time. He tells of the instruction he received from his deceased cousin, Randy, who served as a type of guide for Lance while he temporarily passed into the spirit world. He wrote of seeing a temple there and his amazement at the sight.

> A temple? I thought temples were for our world.
> Why would you have a temple here?
> [Randy replied,] "There is sacred work that must be done here, which is different from that performed on earth. These temples also serve as portals to Heaven."[168]

The concept of temples being in the spirit world is very logical to me. Remember Wilford Woodruff's account of meeting the martyred prophet Joseph Smith outside of the temple in the spirit world. (See p. 106.) The Kirtland Temple, and other latter-day temples built since it was constructed, have served more than one purpose. In addition to being the location designated by the Lord where certain sacred and essential ordinances are to be performed, and where sacred meetings of the Lord's leaders are held, such as solemn assemblies, etc., temples are also where the resurrected Lord, Himself, comes to visit and give instruction and direction to his prophets. If this exalted God wants an especially sacred place—a place consecrated to Him on Earth as His house—even "The House of the Lord"— would it not be reasonable to assume that He would also want a place in the spirit world that is especially sacred and consecrated to Him as His house there? After all, as nice and wonderful a place as paradise is, it is not as exalted or special as the Lord's dwelling place in the celestial kingdom. Therefore, it is certainly logical to believe that He would want and deserve such a special and consecrated place as a temple even in paradise in the spirit world.

Consider the following: An ordinance is performed vicariously on Earth for a person before he has accepted it in the spirit world. For that person to know and understand each covenant he later accepts, it would be necessary for one of the following two experiences to occur: (1) He would need to view a "recording" of his proxy doing the ordinance in his behalf; or (2) He would need to personally participate in the spirit world in the same or a similar ordinance, therein accepting those covenants. It is my opinion that he will go through the same presentation of covenants and personally accept the work done for him vicariously on Earth where such physical ordinances must be performed. In either case, such a "viewing of a recording" or "personally participating in a like ordinance" would best take place spiritually in a temple in the spirit world just as it takes place physically on Earth.

People are organized and orderly in all aspects of their spirit-world lives. They go about their respective activities in order, according to their grade and level of righteousness. Families provide the principal organization of the individuals there.

President Jedediah M. Grant explained it this way:

> . . . the order and government that were there! When in the spirit world, I saw the order of righteous men and women: beheld them organized in their several grades, and there appeared to be no obstruction to my vision: I could see every man and woman in their grade and order. I looked to see whether there was any disorder there, but there was none; neither could I see any death nor any darkness, disorder or confusion! To my astonishment, when I looked at families there was a deficiency in some, there was a lack, for I saw families that would not be permitted to come and dwell together, because they had not honored their calling here.[169]

Thus, although the organization of the spirit world is by families, it is necessary for the individual members of those families to be sufficiently worthy to be with others in their families in order for the group (family) as a whole to function together in full and proper order. The classification of the spirit beings in the spirit world is fully based upon their level of purity and obedience to God our Father. The work in which these individuals and families are involved is perfectly organized and orderly. Everything about it will appear entirely natural and proper, for that it is. Said Joseph Smith of this place, "The spirit people there now exist in a place where they converse together the same as we do on the earth."[170]

The people there are more than happy—they are even joyful. Not only are they free from pain and the prospect of death for themselves and their loved ones, they are free from worldly sorrow and cares. Alma succinctly described their condition:

> The righteous are received into a state of
> happiness, which is called paradise, a state of rest, a state
> of peace, where they shall rest from all their troubles and
> from all care, and sorrow.[171]

Brigham Young also spoke of our condition there:

> When we contemplate the condition of man here
> upon the earth, and understand that we are brought forth
> for the express purpose of preparing ourselves through
> our faithfulness to inherit eternal life, we ask ourselves
> where we are going, what will be our condition, what will
> be the nature of our pursuits in a state of being in which we
> shall possess more vigor and a higher degree of intelligence
> than we possess here? Shall we have labor? Shall we
> have enjoyment in our labor? Shall we have any object
> of pursuit, or shall we sit and sing ourselves away to
> everlasting bliss? These are questions that arise in the
> minds of people, and they many times feel anxious
> to know something about hereafter. What a dark valley

and a shadow it is that we call death! To pass from this state of existence as far as the mortal body is concerned into a state of inanition, (sic) how strange it is! How dark this valley is! How mysterious is this road, and we have got to travel along it. I would like to say to you, my friends and brethren, if we could see things as they are, and as we shall see and understand them, this dark shadow and valley is so trifling that we shall turn round and look upon it and think, when we have crossed it, why this is the greatest advantage of my whole existence, for I have passed from a state of sorrow, grief, mourning, woe, misery, pain, anguish and disappointment into a state of existence where I can enjoy life to the fullest extent as far as that can be done without a body. My spirit is set free, I thirst no more. I want to sleep no more, I hunger no more, I tire no more, I run, I walk, I labor, I go, I come, I do this, I do that, whatever is required of me, nothing like pain or weariness, I am full of life, full of vigor, and I enjoy the presence of my heavenly Father by the power of his Spirit.[172]

At the funeral of Aurelia Spencer, he added:

Here we are continually troubled with ills and ailments of various kinds, and our ears are saluted with the expressions, "My head aches," "My shoulders ache," "My back aches," "I am hungry, dry, or tired;" but in the spirit world we are free from all this and enjoy life, glory, and intelligence; and we have the Father to speak to us, Jesus to speak to us, and angels to speak to us, and we shall enjoy the society of the just and the pure who are in the spirit world until the resurrection.[173]

In this paradisiacal part of the world of spirits, nothing is out of order, which is logical, for these neighborhoods are prepared for those who have strived to become like their Eternal Father. His house is a house of order. These are the dwellings of those who have shown themselves approved and accepted by Him. These are they who dwell in . . . mansions, even in the world of spirits. They can know that what awaits them in the kingdom to come following their resurrection and final judgment are everlasting mansions prepared for them in the Kingdom of their God. Imagine, if the temporary mansions in the spirit world are exquisite, what will the permanent ones in the highest level of the celestial kingdom be like?

As spirits become increasingly righteous and obedient, the more beautiful all of these things around them become. Even the appearance of the spirit people there becomes more and more impressive. It is obvious why—these spirits are ever more like God our Father. Their very appearance shows this. He is the Brightest, the One filled with the most light. He is the Most Radiant of all. These aspects of His Glorious Being make Him the most Impressive of all. Those who are most like Him acquire an appearance most like His. The more an individual has been obedient and valiant to the Lord on Earth, the more filled with light—the more radiant—that person and his raiment are in the spirit world.

CHAPTER 21

CONCLUSION

In this book, we have viewed the great plan of salvation our Father in Heaven has established for each of His spirit children. This plan of happiness includes those steps that He, knowing all as He does, knows are necessary for us to experience and accomplish to obtain the greatest possible happiness. We discussed those steps at the beginning of this book.

That great plan of salvation for mankind begins with the pre-existence for each of our Father's children—our pre-existence as spirit children of God, our Father. In that stage, we accepted God's plan to come to Earth to obtain bodies and experience mortality. It required us to pass through a veil of forgetfulness so our earthly experience would require faith on our part to accept and live the commandments the Father had established through His divine Son, Jesus Christ. Our Father and Jesus Christ knew that this faith-requiring plan would be the best path for us to take to achieve the greatest progress and happiness, both on Earth and throughout eternity.

After completing our mortal probationary experience, we die and pass through another veil into the world of spirits. Based upon our faithfulness and obedience to the commandments and prescribed ordinances and covenants with the Lord, we will warrant one of two general areas in the spirit world—paradise or spirit prison.

We focused on general aspects of the spirit world. We had a view of spirit prison, where basically three different types of individuals go. We discussed the wicked—those evil and rebellious persons who have chosen to follow the wishes and bidding of Satan. We also spoke of two levels of the less wicked: those uncommitted to the Lord; and those who have not, or not yet, committed themselves to accept and live the principles and ordinances prescribed by the Lord to inherit the highest kingdom wherein the Father and the Son dwell.

We next viewed the activities and nature of the righteous and their blissful and happy state in paradise, where they rest in the Lord from the cares and suffering of the world.

Next, the Lord will assign us to one of three kingdoms of glory, or for those who have denied the Holy Ghost, to perdition. We have discussed the differences between those final kingdoms in which we will dwell for eternity.

Then follows the resurrection—a universal gift from our Savior and Redeemer, Jesus Christ. Through the resurrection, He "saves" us from everlasting physical death—separation of our spirit from our body. Then comes the final judgment in which the Son, as Supreme Judge, will judge our pre-mortal, mortal and spirit world lives, choices and obedience.

To summarize the most important points we have discussed herein, let us review some quotations from several modern-day prophets.

President Joseph F. Smith declared:

> The spirits of all men, as soon as they depart from this mortal body, whether they are good or evil, . . . are taken home to that God who gave them life, where there is a separation, a partial judgment, and the spirits of those who are righteous are received into a state of happiness which is called paradise, a state of rest, a state of peace, where they expand in wisdom, where they have respite from all their troubles, and where care and sorrow do not annoy. The wicked, on the contrary, have no part nor portion in the Spirit of the Lord, and they are cast into outer darkness, being led captive, because of their own iniquity,

by the evil one. And in this space between death and the resurrection of the body, the two classes of souls remain, in happiness or in misery, until the time which is appointed of God that the dead shall come forth and be reunited both spirit and body, and be brought to stand before God, and be judged according to their works. This is the final judgment.[174]

President Brigham Young declared:

When you lay down this tabernacle, where are you going? Into the spiritual world. . . . Where is the spirit world? It is right here. Do the good and evil spirits go together? Yes they do. . . . Do they go beyond the boundaries of the organized earth? No, they do not. . . . Can you see it with your natural eyes? No. Can you see spirits in this room? No. Suppose the Lord should touch your eyes that you might see, could you then see the spirits? Yes, as plainly as you now see bodies.[175]

The prophet Joseph Smith taught that the post-mortal spirit world is an actual place where spirits reside and ". . . where they converse together the same as we do on the earth."[176]

The apostle Bruce R. McKonkie wrote:

Life and work and activity all continue in the spirit world. Men have the same talents and intelligence there which they had in this life. They possess the same attitudes, inclinations, and feelings there which they had in this life.[177]

Elder McConkie further explained:

Until the death of Christ these two spirit abodes [paradise and hell] were separated by a great gulf, with

138

the intermingling of their respective inhabitants strictly
forbidden (Luke 16:19-31). After our Lord bridged the gulf
between the two (1 Pet. 3:18-21; Moses 7:37-39), the
affairs of his kingdom in the spirit world were so arranged
that righteous spirits began teaching the gospel to wicked
ones.[178]

The relative conditions and state of mind in the two contrasting
spheres of the post–mortal spirit world are described by the following
two statements from the prophet Joseph Smith:

> The spirits of the just are exalted to a greater and
> more glorious work; hence they are blessed in their
> departure to the world of spirits. Enveloped in flaming fire,
> they are not far from us, and know and understand our
> thoughts, feelings, and motions, and are often pained
> therewith.
> The great misery of departed spirits in the world
> of spirits, where they go after death, is to know that they
> come short of the glory that others enjoy and that they
> might have enjoyed themselves, and they are their own
> accusers.[179]

At the December 4, 1856 funeral of Jedediah M. Grant, a
counselor to President Brigham Young, another counselor, Heber C.
Kimball, related President Grant's vision of the spirit world. President
Kimball summarized the vision as follows:

> Jedediah Grant saw the righteous gathered
> together in the spirit world; there were no wicked spirits
> among them. There were order, government, and
> organization. Among the righteous there was no disorder,
> darkness, or confusion. They were organized into families,
> and there was "perfect harmony." He saw his wife, with

whom he conversed, and many other persons whom he knew. There was "a deficiency in some" families, because some individuals "had not honored their calling" on earth and therefore were not "permitted to . . . dwell together." The buildings were exceptionally attractive, far exceeding in beauty his opinion of Solomon's temple. Gardens were more beautiful than any he had seen on earth, with "flowers of numerous kinds." After experiencing "the beauty and glory of the spirit world" among the righteous spirits, he regretted having to return to his body in mortality.[180]

Remember Elder Melvin J. Ballard's declaration about the relative difficulty of effectively repenting while in mortality versus doing so in the spirit world:

> A man may receive the priesthood and all its privileges and blessings, but until he learns to overcome the flesh, his temper, his tongue, his disposition to indulge in the things God has forbidden, he cannot come into the Celestial Kingdom of God—until he overcomes either in this life or in the life to come. But this life is the time in which men are to repent.
>
> Do not let any of us imagine that we can go down to the grave not having overcome the corruptions of the flesh and then lose in the grave all our sins and evil tendencies. They will be with us. They will be with the spirit when separated from the body.
>
> I have said it is my judgment that any man or woman can do more to conform to the laws of God in one year in this life than they could in ten years when they are dead.
>
> The spirit only can repent and change, and then the battle has to go forward with the flesh afterwards. It is much easier to overcome and serve the Lord when both flesh and spirit are combined as one. This is the time when

men are more pliable and susceptible. We will find when we are dead every desire, every feeling will be greatly intensified. When clay is pliable it is much easier to change than when it gets hard and sets.

This life is the time to repent. That is why I presume it will take a thousand years after the first resurrection until the last group will be prepared to come forth. It will take them a thousand years to do what it would have taken, but three score years to accomplish in this life. And, so, we are to labor and have as little to do when we get through with this life as possible.

You remember the vision of the redemption of the dead as given to the Church through the late President Joseph F. Smith. President Smith saw the spirits of the righteous dead after their resurrection and the language is the same as one of the prophet Joseph's revelations– that they, the righteous dead, looked upon the absence of their spirits from their bodies as a bondage.

I grant you that the righteous dead will be at peace, but I tell you that when we go out of this life, leave this body, we will yearn to do a thousand things that we cannot do at all without the body, and how handicapped we will be, and realize then like a man who has suddenly lost both arms and his legs. We will be seriously handicapped, and we will long for the body; we will crave it; we will pray for that early reunion with our bodies. We will know then what advantage it was to have a body.

Then, every man and woman who is putting off until the next life the task of correcting and overcoming the weakness of the flesh are sentencing themselves to that many years of bondage, for no man or woman will come forth in the resurrection until they have completed their work, until they have overcome, until they have corrected, until they have done as much as they can do.

That is why Jesus said in the resurrection there is neither marriage or giving in marriage, for all such contracts— agreements—will be provided for those who are worthy of it before men and women come forth in the resurrection of the Lord, and those who are complying in this life with these conditions are shortening their sentences, for every one of us will have a matter of years in that spirit state to complete and finish their (sic) salvation. And some may attain, by reason of their righteousness in this life, the right to do postgraduate work, to be admitted into the Celestial Kingdom, but others will lose absolutely the right to that glory, all they can do will not avail after death to bring them into the Celestial Kingdom.

The point I have in mind is that we are sentencing ourselves to long periods of bondage, separating our spirits from our bodies, or we are shortening that period, according to the way in which we overcome and master ourselves.[181]

At one time or another, all who ever possessed a body in mortality will be resurrected. Ultimately, the post–mortal spirit world will cease to exist. Why? The Earth having initially been changed from a telestial world to a terrestrial one, will be changed from a terrestrial into a celestial world. It will thereafter serve as the celestial kingdom for the most faithful resurrected beings.[182]

As we near the end of this book, I wish to express to all who read it, that the things quoted herein from both modern and ancient apostles and prophets are true. I firmly believe the experiences and views quoted and summarized from the experiences of other individuals are correct and accurate. They affirm and complement the descriptions provided by those apostles and prophets. It is my desire to encourage each of us to live better than we have been living, to be more faithful and valiant in our testimonies and efforts to live the commandments of the Lord Jesus Christ. I testify to you that He is the

Only Begotten Son of God our Father. He lives today, having atoned for our sins and paid the supreme price in Gethsemane and on Calvary. He then brought about the universal resurrection, a blessing through His grace and love, given to all mankind, whatever their righteousness or wickedness. He has spoken in the past through His chosen prophets. He speaks today in like manner through living prophets. He has re-established His Church on Earth through the instrumentality of the prophet Joseph Smith. Today, He continues to direct His work, which is ". . . to bring to pass the immortality and eternal life of man."[183] He does so today through His re-established church and his living prophets.

In this book, you have been given a view into our next life— our next realm of existence—the world of spirits. This is our next step, *Our Next Life*, in the great plan of salvation of God, our Father.

The prophet Moroni provided the means by which one may know for himself if the Book of Mormon, in which he wrote, is true. He wrote nearly sixteen hundred years ago for the benefit of people in our day who would read that book of sacred scripture. He wrote:

> And when ye shall receive these things, I would exhort you that ye would ask God, the Eternal Father, in the name of Christ, if these things are not true; and if ye shall ask with a sincere heart, with real intent, having faith in Christ, he will manifest the truth of it unto you, by the power of the Holy Ghost.
> And by the power of the Holy Ghost ye may know the truth of all things.[184]

The same counsel applies to each of us concerning the truths written in this book. Ponder Moroni's words and then follow his counsel to know if this book is also true.

In conclusion, consider this. In our life, we have received so much—enjoyed so many blessings on Earth. We have lived such a nice life and enjoyed such great and enjoyable opportunities. What if we find ourselves unworthy of the blessings the Lord has promised to those who are righteous and obedient? Then, in the spirit world and thereafter in one of the lesser kingdoms, we are not allowed to go where the very righteous go. After having such a wonderful life on Earth with so many blessings, opportunities and luxuries, how would we feel to have a sub-standard existence and "forever" there? How would we feel, seeing so many others so far ahead—so far above—us? Would it not be horrible—or worse—to not be with many family members whom we loved so dearly on Earth, but from whom we now must be separated for eternity?

Remember the prophet Joseph Smith's words:

> The great misery of departed spirits in the world of spirits, where they go after death, is to know that they come short of the glory that others enjoy and that they might have enjoyed themselves, and they are their own accusers.[185]

How would we feel when we meet our ancestors who may have been able to see us and understand our thoughts, feelings and actions and be pained therewith?

But most of all, how would we feel when we leave this life and meet our Savior? At that moment, will we focus on expressing our love, praise and gratitude to Him, and feeling His love and satisfaction for us? Or will we be embarrassed—even ashamed—to be in His glorious presence? How would we feel if we must be ashamed because we had wasted our time and opportunities to repent and progress as was—is—our privilege as spirit children of God?

We were sent to Earth to work out our salvation and become as close to how God is as we possibly can. Through Christ's atonement, we can be found worthy to return to our Father's presence and dwell with Him for the rest of eternity—but only if we have applied ourselves in this life—made ourselves better through sincere repentance and obedience.

I repeat my description of the process that I seek to do regularly in my life. Not only will I make the decision to change, but in my frequent and continuing prayers, I will both earnestly ask for His help, AND, I will voluntarily authorize Him to change my heart to bring about all of these changes (and any others I need) in my own character, desires, feelings and personality traits. I will literally turn my will over to Him, for I sincerely desire that I become what He wills me to become. I can do this, for I know without any doubt that His will is, and always will be, to bless me and you with everything good and wonderful that He can, everything that I and you can become worthy to receive from Him.

Think again of all the increased capabilities, the marvelous and beautiful surroundings and the blissful and supremely happy feelings that are available to us for such a long period of "time" in the spirit world, and then forever thereafter. Considering all these wonderful blessings awaiting those who have earnestly sought to be faithful and obedient to the Lord, my hope is that we will determine to live worthy of the incredible rewards promised by our Father that await us in the spirit world—*Our Next Life*.

ABOUT THE AUTHOR

Glen W. Park and his wife, Dianne, have six children who are all married. They currently have seventeen grandchildren.

He is a businessman and attorney. He earned a B.A. in economics from the University of Utah and a Juris Doctorate from the University of Utah College of Law. He has had executive involvement in a number of successful small businesses. In addition, he has practiced law for more than 36 years.

He has completed seven additional books. Three have already been published; the other four are now in the process of final review before publication.

SOURCES CITED

[1] 1 Corinthians 2:9.

[2] John 8:32.

[3] Pratt, Orson, Journal of Discourses, Vol. 2:248, ed. G. D. Watt, F. D. Richards, London, 1855.

[4] Amos 3:7.

[5] Hebrews 12:9.

[6] Ether 3:16.

[7] Alma 41:10.

[8] Ibid.

[9] Abraham 3:22-25.

[10] Alma 32:18.

[11] Zechariah 13:9.

[12] Ecclesiastes 1:11.

[13] Isaiah 25:7.

[14] Matthew 5:48.

[15] Alma 34:34.

[16] Young, Brigham, *Journal of Discourses* 7:333, ed. G. D. Watt, J. V. Long, et al., Amasa Lyman, London, 1860, 379.

[17] John 5:28-29.

[18] Hosea 13:14.

[19] 1 Corinthians 15:22.

[20] John 5:28-29.

[21] Matthew 7:21.

[22] The Doctrine and Covenants 76:51, 59-60, 62.

[23] *Teachings of the Prophet Joseph Smith*, ed. Joseph Fielding Smith, Deseret Book Company, Salt Lake City, 1977, 182.

[24] Ibid., at p. 182.

[25] Smith, Joseph Fielding, *Doctrines of Salvation*, comp. by Bruce R. McConkie, Bookcraft, Salt Lake City, 1955, 2:182-183.

[26] McConkie, Bruce R., in Conference Report, Oct. 1974, 46; or Ensign, Nov. 1974, 35.

[27] The Doctrine and Covenants 76:75.

[28] Smith, *Doctrines of Salvation*, op. cit., 183.

[29] Talmage, James E., *Articles of Faith*, The Church of Jesus Christ of Latter-day Saints, Salt Lake City, 1977, 148.

[30] Talmage, James E., *The Vitality of Mormonism*, 255–56.

[31] Smith, Joseph Fielding, *Church History and Modern Revelation*, The Church of Jesus Christ of Latter-day Saints, Salt lake City, 1947, 1:287–88.

[32] Smith, Doctrines of Salvation, op. cit., 2:296.

[33] Ibid., at Section 76:91.

[34] Ibid., at Section 76:89.

[35] Ibid., at Section 76:103.

[36] Ibid., at Section 76:106, 107, 108, 112.

[37] Ibid., at Section 76:109.

[38] Ibid., at Section 76:37.

[39] Ibid., at Section 76:38.

[40] Ibid., at Section 76:32-37.

[41] John 5:22.

[42] Malachi 4:5; and The Doctrine and Covenants 2:1.

[43] Isaiah 1:18.

[44] See Matthew 11:28.

[45] Matthew 13:38-43.

[46] Matthew 13:47-51.

[47] Smith, Joseph F. *Gospel Doctrine*, Salt Lake City, Deseret Book Co., 1919, 448.

[48] 1 Peter 3:19-20.

[49] 2 Kings 6:11-12.

[50] 2 Kings 6:16-17.

[51] Young, Brigham, *Journal of Discourses*, 3:372, ed. G. D. Watt, Orson Pratt, London, 1856. (Different volumes cited hereafter may have different editors, cities and dates of publications.)

[52] Young, Brigham, *Discourses of Brigham Young*, ed. John A. Widtsoe, Deseret Book, Salt Lake City, 1946, 376-77.

[53] Pratt, Parley P., *Key To The Science of Theology*, Fourth Edition; Liverpool/London, England, Albert Carrington, 1877, 128-129.

[54] Young, *Journal*, op. cit., 3:369.

[55] Pratt, Parley P., *Key To The Science of Theology*, Fourth Edition; Liverpool/London, England, Albert Carrington, 1877, 128-129.

[56] Young, *Journal*, op. cit., 3:371.

[57] *Teachings of the Prophet Joseph Smith*, op. cit., 207.

[58] See Ritchie, George F. with Sherril, Elizabeth, *Return From Tomorrow*, Fleming H. Revell, a division of Baker Book House Company, Grand Rapid, Michigan, 1978, 1997.

[59] *Teachings of the Prophet Joseph Smith*, op. cit., 353.

[60] The Doctrine and Covenants 130:2.

[61] Smith, *Gospel Doctrine*, op. cit., p. 440.

[62] McKonkie, Bruce R., *Mormon Doctrine*, Bookcraft, Inc., Salt Lake City, 1966, 762.

[63] Alma 34:32-34.

[64] Young, *Journal*, op. cit., 7:333.

[65] *Teachings of the Prophet Joseph Smith*, op. cit., 310-311.

[66] Ibid, at p. 326.

[67] Anon., ca. 1805, Boston.

[68] The Doctrine and Covenants 93:28.

[69] Moroni 10:5.

[70] Young, *Journal*, op. cit., 7:240.

[71] Young, *Journal*, op. cit., 4:132.

[72] Snow, LeRoi C., "Raised From the Dead," Improvement Era, Vol. XXXII, No. 12, October, 1929, 973-974.

[73] Johnson, Peter E., "A Testimony," The Relief Society Magazine, Vol. VII, No. 8, August, 1920, 451.

[74] Young, Lorenzo Dow, "Lorenzo Dow Young's Narrative," *Fragments of Experience, (Sixth book of the Faith-Promoting Series),* Salt Lake City: Juvenile Instructor Office, 1882, 27-28.

[75] Young Lorenzo Dow, *Fragments of Experience*, op. cit., 1882, 29-30.

[76] Moses 7:26.

[77] Pratt, Orson, *Journal of Discourses,* op. cit., 2:240, 244.

[78] Young, *Journal*, op. cit., 13:77.

[79] Ibid., at 14:231.

[80] Ibid., at 13:77.

[81] Kennon, "Briant S. Stevens," Helpful Visions (Fourteenth book of the Faith-Promoting Series), Salt Lake City, Juvenile Instructor Office, 1887, 35-36.

[82] Smith, *Gospel Doctrine,* op. cit., p. 440.

[83] Young, *Journal*, op. cit., 14:231.

[84] Pratt, Orson, *Journal of Discourses,* op. cit., 2:247.

[85] Ibid. at p. 247

[86] Kimball, *Journal of Discourses* 4:2, ed. G. D. Watt, S. W. Richards, London, 1857.

[87] Pratt, Orson, *Journal of Discourses,* op. cit., 2:247.

[88] Pratt, Orson, *Journal of Discourses,* op. cit., 2:239.

[89] Ibid., at 2:245.

[90] Tooley, Lawrence E., *I Saw Heaven: A Remarkable Visit to the Spirit World,* Horizon Publishers, Bountiful, *1994, 75-76.*

[91] *Teachings of the Prophet Joseph Smith,* op. cit., 217.

[92] Tooley, *I Saw Heaven,* op. cit., p. 60-61.

[93] Gibson, Arvin S, *Glimpses of Eternity: New Near-Death Experiences* Examined, Horizon Publishers, Bountiful, 1992, 116.

[94] The Doctrine and Covenants 93:36.

[95] **Ibid.,** at 93:24.

[96] **Ibid.,** at 88:40-41.

97 Ibid., at 84:46-47.

98 See *Teachings of the Prophet Joseph Smith*, op. cit. 353.

99 Ibid., at p. 354.

100 Alma 34:32-34.

101 Ballard, Melvin J., "The Three Glories," Mount Ogden Stake *Slogan*, September 2, 1922, 14. Used by permission of The Church of Jesus Christ of Latter-day Saints.

102 Alma 26:12.

103 Romans 6:23.

104 Alma 34:32-34.

105 2 Peter 2:12-15, 17.

106 *Teachings of the Prophet Joseph Smith*, op. cit., 310-311.

107 Parley P. Pratt, *Key to the Science of Theology*, op. cit., 1877, 120.

108 Young, op. cit., 3:369.

109 Moroni 7:17.

110 Ritchie, George F. with Sherril, Elizabeth, *Return From Tomorrow*, Fleming H. Revell, a division of Baker Book House Company, Grand Rapid, Michigan, 1978, 1997. Used by permission of publisher.

111 Ballard, "The Three Glories,", op. cit., 14. Used by permission of The Church of Jesus Christ of Latter-day Saints.

112 Romans 6: 16-17.

113 Alma 34:32-34.

114 Luke 6:37.

115 Matthew 12: 31-32.

116 I Peter 4:6.

117 I Peter 3: 19, 20.

118 Luke 4:18.

119 Isaiah 42: 7.

120 Alma 42: 15, 23, 26, 27, 28.

121 Romans 6: 16-18, 22.

122 Alma 34:34.

123 *Teachings of the Prophet Joseph Smith*, op. cit., 310-311.

124 Alma 40:12.

125 *The Discourses of Wilford Woodruff*, sel. G. Homer Durham, Bookcraft, Inc., Salt Lake City, 1946, 288-289.

126 Smith, Joseph F., "Rights and Order of the Priesthood," in *Collected Discourses*, 3:99. These remarks were made at the conference of the four stakes of Zion in Arizona, held at Pinetop, Apache County, Arizona.

127 Grant, Heber J., *Gospel Standards, sel. G. Homer Durham*, Bookcraft, Inc., Salt Lake City, 1919, 460-461.

128 See Moses 1:39.

[129] The Doctrine and Covenants 138:38-39.

[130] Smith, Joseph F., "Address of President Joseph F. Smith," *Young Women's Journal* 23/3, March 1912, 129-130.

[131] Ibid., at p. 130.

[132] Smith, *History of the Church* 6:306, (1844), Deseret Book, Salt Lake City, 1975.

[133] Smith, *History of the Church* 6:314, (1844), Deseret Book, Salt Lake City, 1975.

[134] Young, op. cit., 6:349.

[135] Young, op. cit., 7:333.

[136] The Doctrine and Covenants 93:27-28.

[137] Moroni 10:5.

[138] The Acts 8:15, 17.

[139] *Manuscript History of Brigham Young, 1846–1847,* comp. Elden J. Watson, Salt Lake City, 1971, 529.

[140] Helaman 4:24.

[141] Tooley, *I Saw Heaven,* op. cit., p. 60-61.

[142] McKonkie, *Mormon Doctrine,* op. cit., 762.

[143] See The Doctrine and Covenants 138:57; and Smith, Joseph F., *Gospel Doctrine,* 5th ed., Deseret Book Company, Inc., Salt Lake City, 1930, 461.

[144] Smith, Joseph F., "The Desert Blossoming as a Rose," in *Collected Discourses*, 3:219. These remarks were delivered at the Tabernacle in Salt Lake City on 8 January 1893.

[145] Anon, Manti, Utah.

[146] Young, *Journal,* op. cit., 3:370.

[147] Smith, *Gospel Doctrine,* op. cit., p. 435, 436.

[148] Smith, Joseph, *Documentary History of the Church*, Vol. II, 379-382.

[149] See Luke 1:5 et seq.

[150] See Mosiah 27:10-24.

[151] Alma 8:15.

[152] See Moses 1:39.

[153] 1 Corinthians 2:9.

[154] John 14:15.

[155] See Grant, *Journal of Discourses,* ed. G. D. Watt, S. W. Richards, London 1857, and also Crowther, *Life Everlasting,* Horizon Publishers, Bountiful, 1954, 1999.

[156] *Sharing the Gospel With Others, Excerpts from the Sermons of President Smith,* Compiled by Preston Nibley, Deseret Book Co., Salt Lake City, 110-111, 1948.

157 See Heber Q. Hale, "A Heavenly Manifestation by Heber Q. Hale, President of Boise Stake of The Church of Jesus Christ of Latter-day Saints," unpublished manuscript.

158 See Gibson, *Glimpses of Eternity:,* op. cit., 116.

159 See Gibson, Arvin, *Echoes From Eternity: New Near Death Experiences Examined,* Bountiful, Horizon Publishers, 1992, 72-73.

160 Grant, Heber J., *Journal of Discourses,* 4:136, ed. G. D. Watt et al., F. D. Richards, London, 1857.

161 See above endnotes: 104, 105, 106, 107 and 108.

162 See Tooley, *I Saw Heaven!,* op. cit., p. 62.

163 Gibson, *Echoes From Eternity,* op. cit., p. 72.

164 See Gibson, *Echoes From* Eternity, op. cit., at p. 190-191.

165 Grant, *Journal of Discourses,* 4:136, ed. G. D. Watt et al., F. D. Richards, London, 1857.

166 See Tooley, *I Saw Heaven!,* op. cit., p. 83-84.

167 Ibid., at p. 85.

168 Richardson, Lance, *The Message,* American Family Publications, Idaho Falls, 2000.

169 Grant, *Journal of Discourses,* 4:135-136, ed. G. D. Watt, S. W. Richards, London, 1857.

170 Smith, *History of the Church,* 6:311, (1844), Deseret Book, Salt Lake City, 1975.

171 Alma 40:12.

172 Young, *Journal,* op. cit., 17:142.

173 Ibid., 14:231.

174 Smith, *Gospel Doctrine,* op. cit., 448.

175 *Discourses of Brigham Young,* op. cit., 376-77.

176 *Teachings of the Prophet Joseph Smith,* op. cit., 353.

177 McKonkie, *Mormon Doctrine,* op. cit., 762.

178 Ibid., at p. 762.

179 *Teachings of the Prophet Joseph Smith,* op. cit., 310-311.

180 Young, *Journal,* op. cit., 4:135-36.

181 Ballard, "The Three Glories," 14. Used by permission of The Church Archives, The Church of Jesus Christ of Latter-day Saints.

182 See McKonkie, Bruce R., *Mormon Doctrine,* Bookcraft, Inc., Salt Lake City, 1966, 762.

183 See Moses 1:39.

184 Moroni 10:4-5.

185 *Teachings of the Prophet Joseph Smith,* op. cit., 353.